their people smile. The rest of the airlines must be asking, what is wrong with these people?! ▪ *I love* **Trade** [...] *ways so warm and welcoming. She alu* [...] *(and is adored for it in return), and is a* [...] *e my* **Container Store***. If I could give it a hug, I would.* ▪ *I use the Internet café there, drink the* **Umpqua** *coffee and sit down and read the paper. Since Umpqua opened, I love going to the bank.* ▪ *Woot!* **USAA** *customer service is AMAZING. If only more businesses took customer service this seriously, our lives would be so much easier.* ▪ **Wegmans***, I love you. I've loved you since I was a toddler riding in the child seat of the cart! Your service is good, your produce is fresh, & you even rent movies. Darling, when can we set the date?* ▪ **Zappos.com** *is my addiction, my obsession. . . . The best part is free shipping both ways! Now if I could only get a job there, I'd be all set!* ▪ *Reason I love* **Zipcar***: a super-friendly, helpful, and playful attitude apparent in everything they do.* ▪ *When I go on* **WestJet** *I don't feel like I'm on an ordinary flight, waiting for it to end. The crew makes WestJet just like home, but on an airplane.* ▪ **Zane's Cycles** *customers get a free lifetime warranty on every bike they buy . . . and . . . there's free Snapple in the fridge and a coffee bar snuggled in the back of the store.* ▪ *I can't live without* **Zara***!!!!!! You give me style without having to look at the price tag. Loving you is easy when you are this chic and cheap!* ▪ *You might think that I'm kind of a funny creature, but I'm here to tell you that* **Custom-Ink** *rocks my world!* ▪ *Ok, I have a complex about being a Lushie, but I'm a dude who loves* **LUSH***!* ▪ *I'm addicted to* **Threadless.com***. I LOVE IT!!!* ▪ *I love* **USAA** *so much that I can't help sing its praises. I'm like that annoying girl who won't shut up about her new boyfriend.* ▪ *I love you more than life,* **Zappos***. Marry me. End the madness.*

"*I Love You* MORE THAN My Dog!"

"I Love You MORE THAN My Dog"

Five Decisions

THAT DRIVE EXTREME CUSTOMER LOYALTY
in Good Times and Bad

Jeanne Bliss

Portfolio

PORTFOLIO
Published by the Penguin Group
Penguin Group (USA) Inc., 375 Hudson Street, New York, New York 10014, U.S.A. · Penguin Group (Canada), 90 Eglinton Avenue East, Suite 700, Toronto, Ontario, Canada M4P 2Y3 (a division of Pearson Penguin Canada Inc.) · Penguin Books Ltd., 80 Strand, London WC2R 0RL, England · Penguin Ireland, 25 St. Stephen's Green, Dublin 2, Ireland (a division of Penguin Books Ltd) · Penguin Books Australia Ltd, 250 Camberwell Road, Camberwell, Victoria 3124, Australia (a division of Pearson Australia Group Pty Ltd) · Penguin Books India Pvt Ltd, 11 Community Centre, Panchsheel Park, New Delhi - 110 017, India · Penguin Group (NZ), 67 Apollo Drive, Rosedale, North Shore 0632, New Zealand (a division of Pearson New Zealand Ltd) · Penguin Books (South Africa) (Pty) Ltd, 24 Sturdee Avenue, Rosebank, Johannesburg 2196, South Africa

Penguin Books Ltd, Registered Offices:
80 Strand, London WC2R 0RL, England

First published in 2009 by Portfolio, a member of Penguin Group (USA) Inc.

10 9 8 7 6 5 4 3 2 1

LIBRARY OF CONGRESS CATALOGING IN PUBLICATION DATA

Bliss, Jeanne.
"I love you more than my dog" : five decisions that drive extreme customer loyalty in good times and bad / Jeanne Bliss.
    p.   cm.
Includes bibliographical references and index.
ISBN 978-1-59184-295-8
1. Customer loyalty. 2. Customer relations—Management. I. Title.
HF5415.525.B57 2009
658.8'343-dc22   2009017775

Printed in the United States of America
Set in Filosofia

This one's for you, Dad.
I miss you.

Contents

Foreword   xi

Colleen Barrett, President Emeritus, Southwest Airlines

Introduction   1

Chapter One   7

Your Decisions Reveal Who You Are and What You Value

Your collective decisions tell the story of who you are and what you value. Key decisions expose your true purpose. When customers love you, they won't be able to stop talking about you. But you need to earn the right to their story first. Five key decisions drive devoted customers and business growth.

Chapter Two   25

Decide to Believe

There is no more powerful testament of trust than belief. Beloved companies decide to believe. They believe their people. They believe their customers. And they practice this first by suspending cynicism.

Chapter Three 55
Decide with Clarity of Purpose

Beloved companies are clear about their purpose in supporting customers' lives. In decision making, they align to this purpose, to this promise. It elevates people in working toward a common goal.

Chapter Four 85
Decide to Be Real

The beloved companies shed their fancy packaging. Beloved companies strike a chord with customers. They decide to create a safe place where the personality and creativity of their people shine through.

Chapter Five 113
Decide to Be There

It's an everyday charge up the hill to be there for customers, on their terms. Beloved companies are in the scrimmage every day to earn the right to their customers' continued business.

Chapter Six 141
Decide to Say Sorry

How a company reacts to adversity reflects the humanity of an organization, and shows its true colors more than almost any situation it might encounter. Repairing the emotional connection well is a hallmark of companies we love. It makes us love them even more.

Chapter Seven 173
The Decision Is Yours

What is the story the collective decisions of your organization tell customers, employees, and the marketplace? Are your decisions reflecting what you intended? Beloved companies deliberately decide to craft the story they tell. What's your story?

The Final Word 195
Tony Hsieh, CEO, Zappos.com

Acknowledgments 197

Index 201

Foreword

Frankly, when I read Jeanne's draft of *"I Love You More Than My Dog"* the first time, I was somewhat jealous that she had put her thoughts on paper before I'd had a chance to do so. With very few exceptions, almost every thought, every lesson, and every summary could have been about the beloved company for which I carried the customer service torch for close to 37 years (I retired in July 2008).

The second time I read it, I thought, Geez, Louise, this woman shares my long-held belief that intangibles are more important than tangibles, and she instinctively and intuitively "gets it" that Golden Rule behavior must be a way of life for organizations to be successful—as opposed to the "program of the week" to win over customers.

I wholeheartedly subscribe to Jeanne's conclusions about what it takes to earn extraordinary customer loyalty; and through the five decisions that she has selected and the real-life stories she tells about real-life companies, she will convince the skeptics that even they have reason for reading this book. I also share the thought that your collective decisions tell the story of who you are, albeit a person, a business, or an organization; and that to earn the respect (and eventually love) of your customers, you first have to respect those customers. That is why Golden Rule behavior is embraced by most of the winning companies/organizations Jeanne has covered in her easy-to-read and enjoyable book.

In all honesty, I haven't found myself nodding my head in agreement as often to the delightfully simple (but powerful) thoughts expressed in a book since I read *Atlas Shrugged* by Ayn Rand back in 1962! I believe in this book! I believe that Jeanne has captured the spirit, dedication, and passion for causes to which the companies she has highlighted are so totally committed, and I would enjoy the opportunity to meet every person she has told us about in this fun book. We would have a great campfire session telling marvelous exemplary customer service stories and I bet we would laugh and cry over many of them. I found Jeanne to be a kindred spirit and I'm sure I would feel the same way about most of the people she profiles in this book.

If you are looking for a dry, drab college textbook, or a book where you have to look up every other word in the dictionary to understand what is being said, *"I Love You More Than My Dog"* is not for you. If you are dedicated to a cause that you feel could make the world or a town or an organization or even yourself a better place/person, and you just want some commonsense, practical approaches as to what causes people to believe in you and to want to tell your story, then *"I Love You More Than My Dog"* is a MUST READ. I'd be willing to bet that you will find yourself nodding over and over in agreement with the conclusions that Jeanne draws, and I double bet that you will read the book more than once and share it with many of your friends. Enjoy!

Colleen Barrett
President Emeritus, Southwest Airlines
February 9, 2009

"*I Love You* MORE THAN My Dog!"

Introduction

This book is about earning the right to have customers tell your story. When you make decisions that respect and honor customers, you will earn their admiration; eventually even love. Then customers will begin to grow your business for you.

The title of this book, *"I Love You More Than My Dog,"* is a reminder that people are bound by emotion to the things they love. They are bound by emotion to *behaviors* they love. What binds dog lovers to their pets is the constant devotion they receive from them: a warm welcome, caring nature, and selfless actions. All character traits we value in people, *especially* when we come across them in business.

When customers love you, they'll not only turn to you when a particular product or service is needed, they'll turn to you *first*, regardless of the competition. They will tell your story, forming an army of cheerleaders and publicists urging friends, neighbors, colleagues, even strangers to experience your company. The accolade "I love you more than my dog" is a high aspiration. What customers say about the companies they love gets pretty close to that sentiment. The endpapers of this book are filled with comments made by customers proclaiming their love for companies and the people in them. At Yelp, Facebook, Epinions, Twitter, chat rooms, and hundreds of other Web sites every day, people are not bashful to tell stories about how they feel when they are treated well. Customers who love you won't be able to stop raving about you. But you have to earn the right to their story first.

So many companies want to know "How can we get there?"—"How do we achieve a state of being loved that way by customers?" The answer is this: the decisions you make will take you there. Making the five decisions in this book will help you to earn the right to have your story told. They will drive the behaviors customers love.

Are Customers Saying They Love You?

This book is organized to take you on a journey to discover the story of your company being told by customers in the marketplace, as defined by your decisions. It will help you to understand what you are telling customers every day about who you are and what you value because of the actions that come from your decisions. And it will help you adjust your course if your course needs changing.

Moving through the five decisions commonly made by beloved companies, the chapters are filled with examples, both hard and not so hard, that these companies have made. After each profiled decision are questions to challenge you and your organization, to help you reflect on how you would make that decision inside your organization.

Like most of the best leaders I've met in my life who asked more questions than they gave answers, I planned this book to be a reflective journey, so that you can gain a greater understanding about what helps or hinders your bond with customers. Rather than giving you a "one size fits all" solution, my goal was to provide you with the right questions to evaluate and understand your business from your customers' point of view. These questions will lead you to answers best suited for *your* business, for *your* people, and for *your* customers.

What you will find as you traverse this book is that the inside of the clock—the inner workings behind the scenes—is different in the beloved companies. The intent and motivation steering their decisions inspire acts that bond customers to them. To move toward becoming a beloved company is to rethink how you make decisions. Helping you reconfigure how your company makes decisions that impact customers is what I want to provide you in this book. It is one of the best ways I know to help you become beloved.

You can use this book to ask yourself, "What do our decisions say about who we are and what we value?" Use it to understand the intent and motivation behind your decisions today and how they compare to those which resonate with employees and customers: ones that drive their growth and prosperity. And use this book to make a choice. Show your customers you deserve their business by deciding how you will run yours.

Use This Book to Make a Choice.
Make an Active Decision About How You Will Run Your Business.

A great privilege of my professional life is to have been a part of turning the wheels behind some of the most beloved decisions in retailing. Fate delivered me to Lands' End and the Wisconsin farmlands in 1983 as the trainer and confidante of the Lands' End phone reps who took customer orders and served them. Within a year of my arrival, founder Gary Comer invited me to report to him and the company's executive committee. Gary described my job as nurturing the "conscience" of the company through the decisions we made as we grew. During this time, the catalog industry was in its infancy. We experienced 20 to 30 percent growth per year, and the company's passionate stand was that long-term growth was dependent on retaining our strong emotional connection with customers.

Clearly the world and Lands' End have changed since I was there. However, the lessons that built that business travel with me wherever I go. Our decisions revealed our values. Our actions that came from those decisions revealed who we were as people. They told our story. And that story pulled employees and customers toward us. Those uncommon decisions fueled our growth. They drove actions that made us so beloved that we assembled a "Correspondence Corps" of over 200 employee volunteers to answer all the "I love you, Lands' End!" mail we received each month. Our "moment of greatness" was being able to make the decisions that allowed those uncommon actions to occur.

There are many decisions we made during that time that nudged Lands' End along to becoming a beloved company. Here is one decision that especially impacted all of us there because of the intent and motivation behind it, and because of the humility that accompanied its delivery. It gave me faith that business leaders can gracefully blend commerce with their humanity.

In 1989, after many prosperous years, founder Gary Comer decided to personally thank the people of Lands' End for helping him build the business. When customers described Lands' End and why they loved the company, their most frequent comment was "The people who take care of me at Lands' End make me love you." So Gary decided to thank the people who made such an impact on customers that the company grew and prospered. He took $10 million out of his own pocket and built an employee health club that rivaled the best of any in the world. Constructed on the Lands' End campus, it was a gift to our well-being. It was Gary's tribute to our collective decisions that built the business. It was a love letter in the form of a building.

For Gary, the **intent** behind his decision to build that health club was to give back to the southwestern Wisconsin people who had become the face and personality of Lands' End. How they interacted with customers, how they cared—the decisions they made—set Lands' End apart for customers and made it grow. As the company grew, Comer personally benefited and wanted to take good care of the employees who worked alongside him.

His **motivation** for paying for the health club was that he wanted to make the gesture personal—a gift from him and his family to the people of Lands' End. That's why Gary funded it out of his own pocket; it was not a corporate expense. Knowing and understanding what guided Comer's actions—the intent and motivation behind them—is to understand what made them noble.

The Moment of Greatness Is *Not* the Action.
It's the Decision That Allows the Action to Occur.

I close with the story of the dedication of that health club in Dodgeville, Wisconsin, in 1989. On that cold winter day, we trudged through the snow and across the parking lot. Nearly 2,000 of us streamed into the new building. Included in our group were the customer phone reps who began their days at home on their farms at 3 A.M., haying fields and prodding eggs from the underbellies of warm hens before coming to work at Lands' End. They were the kind voices on the other end of the line when someone called, no matter what time of the day or night. The people we called "pickers" were there. They spent their days pushing gargantuan shopping carts up and down the warehouse aisles, filling them up to complete customers' orders. And the "packers" were there. They boxed everything up, making sure customer orders got on the trucks and safely on their way. All the behind-the-scenes people were there too—those who worked throughout Lands' End to make our moments of connection with customers a reality.

We were all ushered into the pool area of this building commissioned as a gift to us. What happened next will stay in my mind for the rest of my life. Gary Comer, the founder of Lands' End, calmly asked us all to walk to the tiled wall at the southeast end of the pool. "This center is dedicated to you," he said, "because it is your passion and love and work that has made all of this possible."

"Find your name," he said. For months, an artist had been at work hand-lettering each of our names onto the tiles covering the wall in front of us. Because we mattered. Because we counted. Because we had achieved something much greater than putting turtlenecks on the backs of millions.

With each shipment, with each call we took, with each box we packed, a bit of who we were also went out the door. And that struck a chord with customers. Because of who we were as people. And because of the decisions that we made about how to treat our customers. Decisions made by simply treating customers how we'd want to be treated ourselves. As I traced the lettering of my name on one of those tiles, shivers went down my spine. I was a part of this.

I can still see that tiled wall with all of our names on it. It's where I got faith that companies have the ability to do the right thing for employees and the customers they serve. It begins with how they make decisions. It's about the intent and motivation that guide them.

Use This Book to Guide Your Decisions.
Tell Your Story of Who You Are and What You Value.

1

Your Decisions Reveal

WHO YOU ARE *and* WHAT YOU VALUE

It's not hard to make decisions when you know what your values are.

—ROY DISNEY

Beloved companies decide differently than everybody else. Acutely aware of how their every action impacts how customers feel and respond to them, they take the time to make purposeful decisions about the contacts they have with customers. Beloved companies make a choice. They actively decide to connect who they are as people with the decisions they make in how they run their business.

Intent and motivation guiding a decision's outcome set people—and companies—apart. And that intent and motivation tell a story, about the people behind the decision and about what is important to them. The common denominator among beloved companies is that they consistently find a way to weave their humanity into the way they make decisions. They never lose sight of the people impacted by them.

Customers admire the beloved companies for how they are *treated*, not for how they are *handled*. And they love these companies because of how they feel when they come into contact with them. The language on the packing slip seems as if an old friend wrote it, not a computer. The voice on the other end of the line asks about your mom for whom you're buying a sweater. And there's no "corporate" pomp when you walk in the door. How beloved companies make decisions inspires acts that transcend normal business practices to create an emotional connection with their customers.

Your Collective Decisions Reveal Who You Are and What You Value.

When you make a decision, it results in an action. And the accumulation of those decisions and actions become how people describe you and think of you. It becomes your "story."

What is the story that the collective decisions of your organization are telling your customers, employees, and the marketplace? What's important to you? Are your decisions reflecting what you intended and what your company stands for? Getting customers to love you begins with how you consider the people impacted by your decisions. You tell customers every day how much you honor them through how you direct decisions in one direction or another. And that's what they play back to the masses. That's what shows up on the Internet.

This book is filled with decisions made by beloved companies of every size and across many industries who earned the right to their customers' stories. They are called *beloved* companies because of the emotional attachment customers have to them.

Common to all of these companies is the concentration, angst, and passion that they put into decision making. Suspending their fear that the dollars and cents won't come swiftly enough, beloved companies decide to run their businesses with what each of us learned as kids—the Golden Rule. And as a result, as you will see in this book, they grow and prosper. Their customers who love them make them grow.

The Humanity in All of Us.

Every day we make a hundred decisions that mark our place in the universe. As individuals, our decisions create the paths of our lives: where we choose to go to school, the person we choose to date, how we decide to deal with adversity and people who do or do not agree with our point of view. All of these things define who we are. They nudge us along to who we become.

When we are young, we learn the Golden Rule. We wholeheartedly believe in it. We do our best to apply it in our lives. Then we strap it to our backs and take that belief with us into business.

The Golden Rule we learned as kids is believed to have always existed in some form. One of Homer's characters in *The Odyssey* said, "I will be as careful for you as I should be for myself in the same need." In the sixth century BCE, Confucius said, "One should not extend harm to others which one would not wish for one's self." The Torah cites, "Love thy neighbor as thyself." In Islam, Mohammed's Farewell Sermon delivers, "Hurt no one so that no one may hurt you." Matthew 7:12 from the Bible gives us "Do to others what you would have them do to you."

The decisions we make in our business lives measure the depth of our humanity—our ability to apply that simple Golden Rule. How we choose to correct something that goes wrong, how steadfast we are in delivering the goods, ensuring quality, and giving people what they need to do these things all expose what we value. The actions that tumble from these decisions expose the kind of people we are.

As we experience companies throughout our lives as both customers and employees, why do we feel so connected to some and distanced from others? Does how we feel about companies relate to our natural desire to follow the Golden Rule? When a company makes genuine attempts to do the right thing, does this draw us to them?

"When we are young, we learn the Golden Rule. . . .

"Then we strap to our backs and take that belief with us into business."

As it turns out, there is a connection. Donald Pfaff, who heads the Laboratory of Neurobiology and Behavior at Rockefeller University, and is the author of *The Neuroscience of Fair Play: Why We (Usually) Follow the Golden Rule*, has proven that we are naturally programmed to treat others as we'd like to be treated ourselves.

We are programmed to care. We naturally want to do the right thing. As employees, we are drawn to companies that allow us to do so. As customers, we become emotionally attached to companies who consider our lives when they make decisions.

Pfaff's findings tell us altruism is a hardwired function of the human brain. We take altruistic actions because a neural mechanism leads us naturally down this path. This creates a tendency for serving the best interest of others. It's our internal wiring for being empathetic—for treating others like we'd like to be treated ourselves. Pfaff tells the story of a man who saw someone fall onto the tracks of a New York City subway. On instinct, he jumped into the well of the tracks, hoisted the stranger onto his back, and carried him to the edge of the platform to be lifted out. Why did he do it? What made him risk his life for someone he did not know? He did what came naturally. His actions were congruent with his instinct to jump in and save the man stranded in the tracks. He was programmed to do the right thing and he did it.

We take that instinct to do the right thing with us to work, except that instead of jumping onto tracks, we want to exercise our instincts for making decisions that are right for customers and coworkers. Beloved companies let their employees exercise that natural instinct. It's part of daily decision making to do what's right. It's decision making that is enabled, heralded, and celebrated—not challenged, impeded, or stopped.

University of Zurich researchers agree that we are "wired" to take the altruistic path. They revealed that a small area in the brain—in the dorsolateral prefrontal cortex, or DLPFC—is responsible for suppressing natural selfish tendencies. It's crucial to our ability to assess fairness and balance that with our own selfish and materialistic impulses.

"Congruence of heart and habit form the backbone of beloved companies."

Congruence of heart and habit form the backbone of beloved companies. Consistency of *knowing* and *feeling* what is right, paired with decision making that yields to the natural tendencies firing inside us, make these companies beloved inside and out. What drives their decisions is the beating heart. It's the measure of how much the right cortex of the brain is present around the conference table.

Congruence of heart and habit enables beloved companies to make uncommon decisions by considering the needs and emotions of customers. In Pfaff's research, the man who jumped onto the subway tracks took an altruistic action because it was done to truly help someone else. The needs of the man who had fallen on the tracks came first. When companies make decisions considering customer needs, often before their own, they do what comes naturally. And that draws customers to them. It creates an emotional bond. It grows their business.

The Five Decisions Made by Beloved Companies:

As customers and employees, we crave what the beloved companies deliver. They enable people to decide and act from a corner of their brain that is congruent with doing the right thing. In doing so, they build an organization with energy and spirit that draws customers to them. We naturally gravitate to companies and people with whom we connect in a human and sincere manner. We like their story because it's the one we strive to live ourselves.

Here are the five decisions that set beloved companies apart. These five decisions reveal who they are and what they value. They earn the right to their customers' story.

DECISION 1: Beloved Companies Decide to Believe.

"We trust our customers. We trust those who serve them."

Inside the beloved companies, they decide to *believe*. They believe their employees and they believe their customers. And they practice this by suspending cynicism. By deciding to trust customers, they are freed from extra rules, policies, and layers of bureaucracy that create a barrier between them and their customers. And by deciding to believe that employees can and will do the right thing, second-guessing, reviewing every action, and the diminishing ability of employees to think on their feet is replaced with shared energy, ideas, and a desire to stick around.

DECISION 2: Beloved Companies Decide with Clarity of Purpose.

"Our iron-clad integrity and clarity guides the direction of our decisions."

Beloved companies take the time to be clear about what their unique promise is for their customers' lives. They use this clarity when they make decisions so they align to this purpose, to this promise. Clarity of purpose guides choices and unites the organization. It elevates people from executing tasks to delivering experiences customers will want to repeat and tell others about.

DECISION 3: Beloved Companies Decide to Be Real.

"We have a spirited soul, humanity in our touch, and personality that's all ours."

Beloved companies shed their fancy packaging and break down the barriers between "big company, little customer." The relationship is between people who share the same values and revel in each other's foibles, quirks, and spirit. That's what draws them to each other. But it's not easy being real; being this transparent with customers takes guts. And only the companies who really know who they are can be "real" consistently—no matter where customers interact inside the company. They decide to create a safe place where the personality and creativity of people come through. They are beloved by those customers who gravitate to their particular brand of personality.

DECISION 4: Beloved Companies Decide to Be There.

"We must earn the right to our continued relationship with customers."

It's an everyday charge up the hill to be there for customers in the ways that are important to them. And it takes its toll because deciding to be there requires more resources and more work. Beloved companies gladly do the hard work. They're in the scrimmage every day to constantly earn the right to their continued relationships with customers. And they work every day to defend their decisions because they know that with each experience they must earn the right for the customer to return. That starts with deciding to be there when customers need them, on customers' terms.

DECISION 5: **Beloved Companies Decide to Say Sorry.**

"We act with humility when things go wrong.
We will make it right."

How a company reacts to adversity reflects the humanity of an organization, and shows its true colors more than almost any situation it might encounter. Grace and wisdom guide decisions to accept accountability when the chips are down—not making accusations and skirting accountability. Apologizing well and repairing the emotional connection with customers is a hallmark of companies we love. In fact, it makes us love them more. How a company makes decisions to explain, react, remove the pain, and take accountability for actions signals loud and clear what they think about customers and gives an indication to the collective "heart" of the organization. Years of good intentions build up a reserve that makes forgiving the beloved companies who make sincere apologies something customers are open to doing.

"It's the intent and motivation guiding a decision's final outcome that sets people . . . and companies apart."

The fact of the matter is, decisions that earn customer love are not easily reached. Many companies try to copy the actions that result from beloved companies' decisions. But to achieve the same impact, what enabled the decision must exist. You must get beyond the decision itself and possess what lies beneath it. What is the intent at the core of the decision? What motivated leaders and employees to make their decisions? We'll examine the "what" and the "why" behind every decision in this book so you can examine how your company makes decisions that impact customers and employees.

It's the **intent** and **motivation**—the "what" and "why"—behind decisions that bond people with companies. Why did Lands' End offer a guarantee? Founder Gary Comer told me his intent was first to send a strong and indelible message inside the company. "A guarantee means we have to deliver on the customers' terms," he said. And his motivation? It was to give people inside the company ownership of doing the right thing for customers. He didn't want to pen people in with rules and regulations. That one decision guided a host of decisions about product quality, service, and operations. Why did we run ads with strong exclamations about the simplicity of our guarantee? Our intention was clear, understood, and delivered on throughout the company in every interaction—to build customer peace of mind. Catalog shopping was in its early stages and people needed to know that we were trustworthy—that a guarantee in our book was a guarantee, with no "ifs, ands, or buts."

Throughout this book, both the intent and motivation behind every profiled decision is explained. When your intent (what you want to accomplish) and your motivation (the reason you make your decision) are driven by your awareness of and empathy for the people impacted by your decisions, the outcomes will set you apart. The humanity and empathy of your decisions will connect you emotionally with customers. And those customers will grow your business by telling the story of their experiences to everyone they know.

Those noble decisions I first experienced at Lands' End inspired its unique culture, from its early days of few employees to the many thousands who have come to work there. They enabled uncommon acts of kindness that marked our place in the world. As transplants from other cultures came into the business, they had only to sit in a few meetings to know what behaviors and habits to model when deciding what to do.

It wasn't just that we were proficient in the business of producing, picking, packing, sorting, and shipping. Who we were as people came through loud and clear in how we acted. The reflection of our humanity *was* mirrored in those decisions. Our decisions were guided by a simple statement that is easy to say but hard to execute: "What's right for the customer is right for all of us."

An incident regarding a shipment of Lands' End turtlenecks shows what we were made of in terms of honoring this commitment. We had shipped thousands to customers, and then found later in the quality review process that some were flawed. Without waiting for customers to contact us, we sent every single customer who had ordered a turtleneck a note: "The turtleneck we originally sent you may have a flaw in it. We're not sure, but we just inspected some that weren't up to our standards, and wanted to make sure that you've got a good one. So just call us if you want a replacement. Don't bother returning the first one we sent. It's on us." We always signed our letters, "Your friends at Lands' End." Your friends. There was a lot of meaning in those two words. We meant it.

Our "customer" was almost mystical to us. The fact that we took orders over the phone or through the mail meant that we didn't know our customers face-to-face. We envisioned what they were going through in their daily lives. We pictured how they felt when they hung up the phone after placing an order; we imagined them opening the door for the delivery man, and the feeling of stretching a brand-new turtleneck over their heads. We took the job of creating an emotional experience when the box was delivered to customers' homes very seriously. How customers felt when they opened it was our report card.

Delivering on this level of commitment gave us a "living" company manual: something with much more impact than any set of words on paper or mission statement about focusing on customers. We were shepherded through the process of learning how to err on the side of the customer. And then were simply trusted to make decisions ourselves in our corner of the world. This internal trust of employees for doing what's right for customers is often lost in business today. It is teaching by example, not by policy. And it is the only way that employees trust the commitment and feel inspired to model the actions that set the beloved companies apart from the rest of the pack.

What Story Do Your Decisions Tell About You?

Making the right decisions to tell a story you're proud of begins with holding up a mirror to yourself and your organization. You need to ask the right questions to review your current decisions and understand the story they reveal about you today. You need to know the important decisions to make for the future.

Darwin Smith, CEO of Kimberly-Clark from 1971 through 1991, is considered by many to be one of the top ten CEOs of all time. Jim Collins, in his book *Good to Great*, introduced the story about how Smith moved his company from a languishing business to the world's highest performing paper-based consumer products company, by asking questions and moving rocks.

In 1971, when he took over the helm of Kimberly-Clark, Smith worked to grasp what direction to take the company. In the quiet of the evening at his Gotrocks Farm in Wisconsin, he would contemplate the situation by unearthing rocks on his property and moving them into piles. When his wife Lois heard the scrape of a backhoe in the middle of the night, she knew he was thinking over a decision. In the morning, the extent of his thinking would stand in large piles of rocks that had been moved from one pile to another as he contemplated his course of action.

Those evening sessions didn't bring Smith answers; they brought him questions. Questions he would ask his leadership team and people inside his company for months. He wanted to know what Kimberly-Clark should stand for, what it could be known for, and how it could grow financially.

The answers to his questions told Darwin Smith the story of his company. Smith learned where Kimberly-Clark stood and what decisions and actions had been made to get the company to its current position. From those answers, Smith realized what initial actions he needed to take to move the company in a new direction. The answers to Smith's questions led him to his first steps in leading Kimberly-Clark onto the path of its success.

This Book Is Your Set of Questions for Understanding the Story of Your Company.

To begin to move forward, you need to review the decisions you've made about customers and employees that have brought you to where you are today. This book is your springboard.

This book will lead you on a path of discovery similar to the one Darwin Smith followed with his rocks and his questions. Through this process, he accomplished three things. First, he determined the right questions to ask. The answers to those questions then told him the story of his company. And third, that story led him to his course of action.

Your path of discovery in this book will lead you to understand how the decisions of your business have impacted your relationships with customers and employees. And it will give you the questions to ask yourself and your organization about how to change your course if your course needs changing. Each chapter focuses on one of the five key decisions made by beloved companies. Eight to ten companies' decisions are profiled in each chapter to show how they applied them in running their businesses. Following each profiled decision, challenge questions are posed to you—so that you can consider how *you* would make that decision in the same situation.

These questions will help you understand the intent and motivation behind your decisions and how they compare to those that resonate with employees and customers of beloved companies, driving their growth and prosperity. Connecting your answers will tell you how you are seen from the outside looking in. The sum of your answers throughout this book will connect to tell you the story of who you are and what you value as defined by the decisions you make and the actions that tumble from them.

The final chapter lists all of the questions in the book sequentially, so that you can work through them with your organization to diagnose the strength of your current relationships—as told by the decisions you make to run your business.

The Impact of Being a Beloved Company.

There is an effect that noble decisions have on a company and its people and its customers. They always seem to find a way back to their "sender," to those who make them. Meaning, yes, they deliver financially. Having a clear path for decision making is one of the most potent arrows in the quiver of beloved and prosperous companies. Beloved companies enjoy a personal relationship with their customers and employees that transcend others. Their connections are genuine. In the pages of each of the coming chapters you will see just how substantially these good decisions yield business growth and financial results.

But noble decisions also deliver beyond financial definitions of prosperity. The decisions of beloved companies create prosperity of the human spirit. Their decisions yield outcomes and actions that draw people to them. Employees stay and become increasingly valuable to the business. Customers become the army that makes them known and beloved in the marketplace.

They Retain Happy, Engaged Employees.

Running their businesses with lower recruiting costs and an engaged workforce are common denominators of beloved companies. At Griffin Hospital in Derby, Connecticut, loved for how they treat patients and employees, 6,483 people applied for 44 open positions in 2008. In healthcare, where quality workers are scarce, this is testament to the pull that Griffin has in the marketplace. Wegmans Food Markets, Inc. trusts the people working in the stores to make their own decisions about how to keep the promise that "No Customer Goes Away Unhappy." Of the almost 6,000 Wegmans employees, about 20 percent have ten or more years of service. This grocery store receives more than 150,000 applicants per year who want to wear its aprons. Beloved companies make decisions that tell this story to their employees: "We honor you, we respect you, and you are valuable to this business."

Customers Are Their Biggest Champions; They Participate in the Business.

There are over 200 YouTube videos of Zipcar customers with "their" cars. Threadless.com has grown tenfold from 70,000 members at the end of 2004 to more than 700,000 members in 2008. Their customers submit designs for the T-shirts they sell and vote to determine which are produced. The Harley Owners Group started in 1983 now has 850,000 members, many of whom have the Harley-Davidson logo, the number one logo requested in the world, tattooed on their body. Nearly all of these companies have "fan" Web sites that have sprouted up from devoted followers. For example, ikeafans.com celebrates frugal and creative approaches for decorating one's home. Customers at fan sites zipkarma.com and lushies.com chat about the products they love, providing suggestions and feedback to company members who frequently chime into the conversation. In 2001, after the terrorist attacks in the United States, Southwest Airlines received thousands of letters from customers who wanted to make sure that Southwest would stay in business so they could continue flying with them. Many customers included checks with their letters. Some customers returned travel vouchers they had received.

Customers Beg for Them to Be in Their Lives.

In 30 minutes of Internet searching, I uncovered petitions from the cities of Portland, Maine; Washington, DC; Nashville, Tennessee; Palm Springs, California; and Albany, New York, begging the Trader Joe's corporate headquarters to open a store in their community. Bruce Roter of Albany, who led the grassroots campaign there, stepped up campaign efforts after he received a letter from the company saying no plans exist for a store right now. Not deterred by the rebuff, he and others on his committee responded by sending postcards of the city—complete with drawn-in arrows showing just where their store would fit right in—to Trader Joe's to demonstrate what a beautiful site it would be for them. In another city, an open letter sent to the *Baltimore Business Journal* addressed to the corporate folks at Trader Joe's was titled "Please, Please Open a Store in Baltimore." Over 2,000 signatures accompanied the request.

Customers Swarm Their Openings.

When IKEA opens a store, traffic must often be rerouted and dozens of police officers engaged to help manage the crowds. At its November 2007 Orlando, Florida, opening, people camped out for 48 hours prior to the event. Three hundred and fifty employees manned the store that day, preparing for the several thousand who would eventually go through. In September 2008, amidst one of the bleakest periods in retailing, Zara opened a new store in Skokie, a Chicago suburb, without advertising. Word of mouth alone brought in droves of women. Some took the day off work. Others drove hours to reach one of the first Zara stores in the Chicago area. Zara's customers tell their story and fuel their growth. In September 2007, the Trader Joe's that opened in Bellingham, Washington, had more than 2,000 people go through checkout on opening day.

Customers Fuel Their Growth.

In August 2008, Zara eclipsed Gap to become the world's largest clothing retailer because of its decision to keep customers coming back with current and ever-changing inventory. Zara keeps their prices low and their customers begging for more because of how they've decided to design, produce, and distribute. Internet clothing and shoe retailer Zappos.com grew from gross merchandise sales of $1.6 million in 2000 to over $1 billion in 2008 because of how they stayed true to their core; they stuck to decisions they made when they were a fledging Web site and kept to them as they grew. Even what some consider the last harbinger of "service," the technology sector, can grow when decisions connect heart and habit, yielding enviable growth and profitability. Web services company Rackspace has achieved 50 percent annual growth by practicing these decisions. The common denominator for all of these companies is how they make decisions which embrace and connect them to customers—decisions *you* can make in your own business.

Customers Want to Stay in Touch with Them Personally.

Tony Hsieh, CEO of Zappos.com, has hundreds of thousands of people following him on Twitter. Why do people follow Tony? Because they know that he actually sends his own "tweets," and they like following him in his daily life. Zappos folks scour the Internet daily to see when they show up in blogs and then personally respond. Recently, a love letter to the company showed up on a Web site called suggestionbox

.com. The message simply was, "To Zappos: keep doing what you are doing. I love Zappos and free shipping and quick delivery." Zappos replied, "We love you too! Thank you for taking the time to enter this comment and make our day!" Mark Constantine, founder of LUSH cosmetics, volleys spirited conversations with "Lushie" fanatics around the world on their open forums. Here they give him spirited feedback about LUSH and their experiences, beg to keep products that are slated to be eliminated, and talk about life in general. Last count on the North American forums was 1,158,396 posts.

Use This Book to Guide Your Decisions. Tell the Story of Who You Are and What You Value.

When customers love you for what you do and how you do it, they will tell your story. They'll want people to get to know you and your actions and your decisions. Customers are proud to compel others to try the businesses they love. Customers who love you will market for you more powerfully than you can possibly market yourself. And your customers will grow your business.

What Decisions Will You Make to Become "Beloved"?

In a world that is spinning so fast, we crave what the beloved companies deliver. Beloved companies share this set of five active and purposeful decisions which inform and motivate their conduct. They decide to believe. They decide with clarity of purpose. They decide to be real. They decide to be there. They decide to say sorry. The simplicity of these five decisions belies the rigor and passion by which they are reached and need to be defended. All of the beloved companies make these humanity-defining decisions, which set the course of their businesses and earn the right to their customers' devotion, and to their story.

Use the decisions in this book to understand the intent and motivation behind your decisions and how they compare to those that resonate with employees and customers, driving growth and prosperity. And use them to make a choice. Make an active decision about how you will decide, about what you decide. About what you want your story to say about who you are and what you value. Are you ready?

The Decision Is Yours.

2

Decide to **BELIEVE**

Show me the person you honor, for I know better by that the kind of person you are.

For you show me what your idea of humanity is.

—THOMAS CARLYLE

I believe you. With those three words, we honor the recipient. We give up control and return it back to the sender. Inside the beloved companies, they decide to believe. Trust and belief are cornerstones of their relationships. By deciding to trust customers, they are freed from extra rules, policies, and layers of bureaucracy that create a barrier between them and their customers. And by deciding to believe that employees can and will do the right thing, second-guessing, reviewing every action, and the diminishing ability of employees to think on their feet is replaced with shared energy, ideas, and a desire to stick around.

There is an energy that comes from being believed, from being trusted, and from sending that trust back to customers and employees. I felt it at Lands' End. At that time, the description I used was that "it was like coming home." For me and others that meant being in a place that felt unconditional in its nurturing—encouraging the best version of us and our work. We were trusted, more was expected of us, and we stretched to deliver it. "The opportunity to realize full potential as a person" is how the MIT Sloan School of Management's *A Study of Spirituality in the Workplace* defines that elusive feeling. When our intelligence, creativity, emotions, and humor blend to inform our conduct without reservation, we realize our full potential. Others' belief in us and in our ability fuels this achievement.

Too often in our daily lives, it feels as if businesses hold all the

> "I believe you. With those three words, we honor the recipient."

cards. As employees, we are penned in by rules and regulations which seem to define our every move. As customers, we fear we don't know the rules. Or worry that we aren't following them. And sometimes even worse, that we will not be believed.

Let's say you have purchased a shirt, never worn, that you need to return. As the bag is handed over the counter and the salesclerk gives it the once-over, why is there an irrational fear that often takes hold, kicking in an instinct to defend yourself for making the return? This is because, as customers, we've come to expect to *not* be trusted. In another example, let's say you are driving your car with your child playing in the backseat. Distracted by the little show going on behind your back, you take your eyes off the road for a minute and experience a fender bender with the car in front of you. You brace for the call to the insurance company that you've been paying for years to cover incidents such as this one. But what do you feel? The first emotion is usually fear that the accident won't be covered, followed by the fear that your story to the auto insurance claims department won't be believed.

Beloved companies grasp that most people strive to do the right thing. They decide to believe. They believe in their employees and they believe their customers.

Beloved Companies Decide to Believe.

"We trust our customers. We trust those who serve them."

There is no more powerful testament of trust than belief. "I believe you" means "I trust you." Beloved companies decide to *believe*. They believe their customers. And they believe those who serve them. Each beloved company makes key decisions that mark its place in the universe with customers. Nurturing the organization first is always among them. That is why so many companies beloved by customers are also beloved by employees. That is why they are the greatest places to work.

Can you put a price on human kindness? On acts of valor? No. But the market values positions by how much people are paid. A nurse's aide earns about $9.93/hour. Erlene Henderson is a certified nurse's aide in the Baptist Healthcare System who saw that the health of one of her patients was declining, in part because her basic dignities and living environment were compromised. On her own time and her own (precious) nickel, she decided to make additional visits to her patient's home, gathering and collecting necessities for her. On one visit, she brought new soap for the bathroom; on another, curtains for the windows. Each individual touch created a moment of tenderness that elevated the dignity of the patient and with that her spirit to fight. Why would someone whose own resources are so precious be inspired to give in this manner? What motivates a company to encourage the front line to rise above standard operating procedure?

Elevating the dignity of patients at Baptist Healthcare begins with deciding to elevate the dignity of those who serve them. It begins because Baptist decides to BELIEVE in the people closest to patients and families. This guides how they hire, train, and develop employees. It's the intent and motivation behind Baptist Healthcare's employee selection that breed trust in the people they select to care for their patients. And it's their belief that memory creation—creating indelible marks of kindness that make people want to return—is most effectively delivered with unencumbered passion. When Baptist Healthcare puts their trust and belief in the people on the front line caring for its patients that belief translates daily to these simple acts of kindness that—to their patients—are uncommon acts of valor.

Beloved companies believe their customers. They give control back to customers by trusting them. They suspend the rules and policies and operate from the belief that customers generally do the right thing. Zane's Cycles, a Connecticut retailer

> **"Elevating the dignity of patients . . . begins with deciding to elevate the dignity of those who serve them."**

selling $13 million worth of bicycles annually from one retail location, will always replace a returned inner tube with no questions asked. This replacement policy is grounded in trust.

Griffin Hospital, a regional hospital also in Connecticut, develops healthcare workers' natural instinct for an open and honest patient relationship. They herald and nurture this instinct to the point of overturning time-honored policies that protect hospitals. One example is their decision to open up medical records to patients and family members who would benefit from seeing patient records, at the risk of potential legal liability. Griffin Hospital made a decision to believe in the goodness of families. Within the guarded healthcare industry, Griffin chose to be guided by relationships of trust. Compare that to other guarded industries, such as financial services, which have a track record of keeping the rules sketchy and details of their relationships buried in fine print. The companies most beloved by customers put everything out in the open. Releasing the control factors that pen people in inspires the imagination of their staffs to do their best work because they are entrusted to come up with solutions on their own. Not surprisingly, people want to work for companies who celebrate and encourage their natural tendencies for helping customers. Trust and belief are the foundation.

By believing that customers who are poor can be trusted, Grameen Bank has boosted millions of impoverished people in Bangladesh, and recently, poor immigrant women in the United States, up and out of their plight. The idea for Grameen Bank began in 1974, when Muhammad Yunus, an economics lecturer at the University of Chittagong in Bangladesh, loaned $27 to 42 Bangladeshi villagers so that they could buy materials to make bamboo furniture. They had no collateral to offer Yunus, but it was such a small loan, he didn't worry. However, those villagers worried about upholding their honor and, of course, repaying every cent. Which they did.

Bangladesh at that time was ravaged with famine and poverty. The small gift that Yunus gave to those villagers was, to them, nothing less than their freedom from a hand-to-mouth existence, allowing them to take control of their lives. Inspired by how such a small amount of money made a significant impact in the lives of the villagers, Yunus implored local banks to help him set up a lending service for the poor. On principle, the banks turned him down. They could not and would not lend money to poor people. They didn't trust them. Muhammad Yunus decided that he would trust and believe in the poor villagers. His solution became Grameen Bank.

The abiding principle of belief underwrites this bank. Based on an honor system called microcredit, the process relies on mutual trust and accountability within small groups of villagers who desire loans. Small five-member groups of individuals must apply together to Grameen Bank when they are in need. The principle behind this is the responsibility of individuals to the group. Two members of the group are offered loans; only if these two members pay back the principal portion of their loans plus interest over six weeks can the other members of the group become eligible for their loans. These loans require no collateral or legal documents. Lending mostly to women (98 percent), Grameen's aim is to improve the lives of loan recipients. To advance this purpose, loan recipients must pledge to take sixteen actions that will improve their lives. One of those sixteen commitments, "We shall send our children to school," has resulted in 100 percent enrollment of Grameen customers' children in schools. Grameen Bank counted on people's dignity and honor as collateral.

With over 7.3 million borrowers in Bangladesh in 2008, and the initiation of loans to poor immigrant women in New York, Grameen Bank's trust and belief are returned to the sender—or, in this case, to the lender. The loan repayment rate is 99 percent—testament to the power of belief and how it can change people's lives.

What Energy Can You Unleash Inside Your Organization by Deciding to Believe?

What follows is the deconstruction of a set of decisions made by companies across diverse industries such as healthcare, e-commerce, financial services, retail, grocery stores, fast-food restaurants, manufacturing, and technology. You'll see the intent of their decisions—what they wanted to accomplish—as well as their motivation for making the decisions.

In uncovering their intention and motivation, what becomes clear is that these companies defy traditional practices and resist restricting customers and employees with a set of rules and regulations. In manufacturing, where friction between workers and management is almost unavoidable, it was reduced by a decision to build a partnership. The belief: that people can meet in the middle, that workers and management are stronger together than apart. In the majority of fast-food restaurants and grocery stores, where worker retention is classically low and staffs are filled with people who just put in their time and leave, beloved companies decide to make staff selection one of the most important things that they do. Their belief: once they hire the right people, they can trust them to live by the values, spirit, and passion for which they were chosen. In healthcare, fear of litigious patients was suspended in a decision to make records available to patients and their families. The belief: trust is reciprocated.

In each of these cases, companies have been able to suspend the cynicism. They have diminished the rules. And instead, they have decided to believe:

- in the good judgment of the people they hire.
- that trust is reciprocated between companies and their customers.
- in the honesty and integrity of their customers.
- that honoring the intelligence of employees grows their business.

What energy can you unleash inside your organization by deciding to believe? How much second-guessing do you signal to your customers and the front line serving them with your rules, regulations, and policies? Are you ready to "skinny down" your policy manual? You will increase your prosperity by deciding to believe in your customers and your people. The decision to believe is core to beloved companies. Having this ability is the foundation for building the kind of company that employees love and customers want to be associated with.

These company decisions that follow demonstrate that the ability to simply "believe" can and should continue to exist in business. I hope they will energize and inspire you. After each profiled decision there is a challenge page for you and your organization that opens with a single question. This lets you stop and consider how you believe now. How you'd like to believe in the future. And, last but not least, how you translate what you believe into how you conduct yourself as a business.

The Decision Is Yours.

Griffin Hospital Decided to Open Up Its Medical Records to Patients.

DECISION INTENT: Honor Patients' Right to Their Information.

Griffin Hospital wanted to have no secrets between themselves and their patient "customers." The traditional approach of doctors or medical professionals delivering only select information often left patients and family members feeling that they were not in control. It put the customer out of power and the medical professional in power. Griffin wanted to balance out that lopsided relationship. They wanted to create a hospital/patient/family partnership. So they decided to make medical records available to patients and their families.

MOTIVATION: Mend Years of Imbalanced Healthcare Relationships.

Through their gesture of making records available to patients, Griffin showed that managing the journey to health was an equal partnership between themselves and patients and their families. They wanted to mend years of a perceived imbalanced relationship, so Griffin made the total transparency of patient medical records an olive branch. Anything the hospital knew, the patient and family could know. In doing so, Griffin Hospital patients could spend all the time they wanted with their records, have them explained, and con-sider them their "own." They could even make comments on their own charts.

IMPACT: Partnership and Trust Replaced Fear and Suspicion. Malpractice Suits Declined.

Worried doctors feared that patients armed with this information would fuel an increase in lawsuits. The total opposite occurred: this decision *reduced* malpractice claims. Patients and families fell into partnership with the medical staff. After Griffin Hospital granted patients and their families access to their medical records, malpractice claims against the hospital dropped by more than 43 percent—from 32 percent in 1996, before the policy was enacted, to 18 percent in 2005. It's noteworthy to add that this reduction in claims dropped during a period of great growth for Griffin Hospital. Patient discharges rose 40 percent during that period, an increase that usually carries an increase in claims. This decision stopped that cycle. Trusting patients with their own records grew patient belief in Griffin Hospital, and ultimately contributed to its growth. Griffin earned an 80 percent referral rate from customers who participated in this new decision. Surely there's a simple gesture you can make to show customers you trust them, that you believe that trust is reciprocated.

Are You TRANSPARENT *with Your* Customers?

What information are you holding close to your vest because it gives you the power?

Is there anything you know that customers could prosper from knowing and understanding?

Do you believe that trust is reciprocated?

Decide to BELIEVE.

The Container Store Decided
to Share Board-Level Financials with All Employees.

DECISION INTENT: Employees Who Feel and Act Like Partners.

The Container Store, which provides storage and organization solutions through an "uber" friendly and helpful retail experience, is a privately held company. Over 3,000 employees work in 47 stores across the United States and in a distribution center and home office in Coppell, Texas. And every single one of them knows the company's detailed financials. The Container Store's hiring philosophy is "One great person equals three good people." So once the company brings someone on board, that person is considered a partner. This partnership commitment with employees equals absolute trust. "The Container Store's goal is to be able to provide all employees with as much information as the executives have," according to Chairman and CEO Kip Tindell. To live up to this promise, two or three times a year its full profit-and-loss status and all other financial topics are shared in a 30-page briefing given to each and every employee.

MOTIVATION: Open Communication Breeds Employee Passion and Partnership.

"The way to retain employees, to make them care, is to communicate everything to them," says Tindell. Knowing the company-wide impact of everyone's efforts on business performance and how the overall business is doing bring an understanding of how each individual impacts the company's growth and marketplace position. Distribution folks know their support to the stores means getting products delivered on time and in good condition. Store folks deliver the customer experience. People at the home office create and source the innovative products that pull customers into the stores. They all connect to fuel the growth of the company. Knowing the details of financial investments in each area and the overall business results connects the dots between each position and each contributor.

IMPACT: Employees Want to Stay and Grow the Company.

By committing to creating an environment of trust and nurturing in their employees, The Container Store has successfully built a retail experience that compels customers to come back for more. Their stable workforce, with only a 15 percent turnover rate, has contributed to the double-digit growth achieved by The Container Store every year since it began in 1978. Achieving $577 million in revenue in 2008, energetic and passionate employees stand behind the store they love. Can you sustain the excitement of your company for customers in this manner, by deciding to honor the intelligence of your employees?

Do You Fan the Flames of Trust?

What actions can you take, or policies can you remove, to show employees you believe in them?

Beloved

companies

throw away

the rule book.

Can you?

Decide to BELIEVE.

W.L. Gore Decided
to Cover Their Customers' Backsides, but Not Their Own.

DECISION INTENT: Inspire Self-Motivation, Not Mandated Performance.

A garment made with W.L. Gore products is probably hanging in your closet somewhere at your home. It's nearly impossible to buy a ski jacket or slicker without seeing the "GORE-TEX" tag hanging from the garment. But W.L. Gore's reach extends far beyond what most of us know, to dental floss, guitar strings, surgical products, and many other categories. Revered for its ability to innovate, W.L. Gore has been named "pound for pound, the most innovative company in America" by *Fast Company*. What lies behind this ability is what founder Bill Gore decided to focus on as he began the business: how people inside the company come to make decisions among themselves. Deciding *how* to decide has driven the growth, ingenuity, and continued innovation at W.L. Gore.

DECISION MOTIVATION: Sustain a Culture of Innovation for the Long Run.

W.L. Gore's ability to drive a culture of continuous innovation rests with its ability to reject traditional hierarchical convention, titles, and rank in its decision making. The company focuses instead on a democratic process in which decisions stick. Founder Bill Gore wanted a company where employees' spirit grew by what they accomplished, not by which corporate scrimmage they had won—where more time was spent generating ideas rather than generating ways to cover one's backside. So he decided to create a "non-organization" approach for his new company that would inspire creativity in its employees. He envisioned a "lattice" structure where people would work interconnectedly with one another rather than through a hierarchy. Gore wanted "leaders" to emerge through the ideas they presented and the commitment received to put ideas into action. "Power" is about ideas and the ability to get them sold.

IMPACT: Sustained Culture, Growth, and Spirit of W.L. Gore Associates.

This radical idea for a culture sticks because Bill Gore's idea honors and upholds the human spirit of the people inside the company. At W.L. Gore, the belief is that people will step up and deliver when they are not regulated. Through a democratic decision and innovation culture, W.L. Gore has grown to a $2.4 billion company. They are one of only five companies that have been on *Fortune* magazine's "Best Companies to Work For" list for twenty-five years, since it was initiated. Do you practice democratic decision making? What energy and innovation could you unleash with democratic decision making?

Do You Practice

Democratic

Decision

Making?

Do the best ideas of your company get to see the light of day? Are good ideas given a chance to prosper, *no matter where they come from?*

Decide to BELIEVE.

Zane's Cycles Decided
Not to Request Collateral for Customer Test Drives.

DECISION INTENT: Let Prospective Customers Know Zane's Values.

With only one retail location, Zane's Cycles of Connecticut is one of the three largest bike shops in the United States. They sell $13 million each year in bicycles, and bike supplies, with a relationship grounded in customer trust. For example, on any given day you might see a $6,000 bike go out the door for a test drive without any one of Zane's folks asking to collect the customer's identification or any type of collateral. "Do you want my license?" is often asked by the customer. The response is always, "Nope, just have a good ride." Zane's makes this decision because they want potential customers to know that in this world there's a store that trusts them, and it's Zane's. Made as a decision to embrace customers, this decision also sends a strong message to Zane's staff. "This is not about protecting ourselves," owner Chris Zane says. "We're in the people business, not the thing business. This decision helps our staff understand and act on that key difference." It gives customers confidence and a lasting impression that they have found a place where they'll want to do business.

MOTIVATION: Each Customer's Lifetime Value is $12,500. Zane's Won't Risk That.

Zane's Cycles decided to act on its belief that the majority of customers do what's right. "We calculate the lifetime value of every customer at $12,500," says President Chris Zane. "Why start out that customer relationship by questioning their integrity? We choose to believe our customers." New Zane's employees often suggest that they protect the business by taking customers' keys or wallets when they test drive a bicycle. Chris Zane firmly says "no" to this suggestion. This is when employees and customers realize Zane's is a service business, not a product business. And it sets the tone for how they interact with people. It frees them to do the right thing.

IMPACT: Trust Is Reciprocated: Zane's Loses Only Five Bikes a Year.

Customers feel trusted by Zane's. And that trust is returned to Zane's. Of the 4,000 bikes they sell each year, only about 5 are stolen during test drives. For Zane's it's just not worth having the whole attitude of the company change because of the attitudes of 5 dishonest people. Zane's believes customers are good. That attitude frees Zane's to grow. They have achieved an average annual growth rate of 23 percent since opening in 1981. Why not take a page from Zane's, and take a hard look at your policies? Change or eliminate any that exist to "protect" you from your customers.

Do You Believe Customers are an ASSET or a Cost Center?

Valuing customers makes it easy to make decisions about how to treat them

It enables your employees to do the right thing for the relationship. It enables the business to invest in customers rather than simply managing costs.

Decide to BELIEVE.

Trader Joe's Decided
That Employee and Customer Taste Buds Rule.

DECISION INTENT: Give Customers and Employees the Power to Select Their Products.
Shopping at Trader Joe's is like going on a treasure hunt for food. Customers smile as they reach for products and become part of the inside joke: Thai-style dumplings are produced by "Trader Ming," and pizza comes from "Trader Giotto." Vitamins are courtesy of (who else?) "Trader Darwin." Charming as those are, what rules at Trader Joe's is how things taste. Trader Joe's decides which items will be carried in its stores based on the palettes of their employee tasting panel in Monrovia, California. At the sound of a maritime bell rung in the main office, the panel breaks from their "regular jobs" and assembles to taste a new batch of products to determine if they should line the shelves of Trader Joe's. The panel tastes the food, has thorough discussions, and then decides what goes into the stores. Once a product makes it to the stores, it goes through the ultimate test: customer tasting. Customers' taste buds have the final say if something stays or something goes.

MOTIVATION: Bond with Customers Through Feedback and Participation.
Trader Joe's believes in their employees to get the products to the shelves and in their customers' feedback to keep them there. "Tasting Huts" throughout the stores offer generous mouthfuls of both new products and old favorites proffered by conversational crew members who don't ever look at you sternly if you take more than one or two tastes. If these new products don't find a customer following validated by tastings and sales, their fate is sealed: they're out. Trader Joe's always rotates out the bottom 10 percent based on customer selection, sales, and feedback. The cornerstone of the Trader Joe's experience, they know, is delivering great food at a good value, with some whimsy thrown in.

IMPACT: Sales Per Square Foot Is Three Times Other Grocery Stores.
By believing in its customers' discerning taste buds to stock its shelves, Trader Joe's has forged an intensely close bond with those customers. Long before other forms of social media took hold, Trader Joe's was giving its customers a vote on what they sell. This belief has spurred on Trader Joe's to become a $6.5 billion supermarket with zealot customers who won't shop anywhere but "their" Trader Joe's. Each Trader Joe's store carries about 3,000 items compared to standard garden-variety grocery stores carrying 30,000 items, yet in sales per square foot Trader Joe's is a force in the industry. It is estimated that Trader Joe's generates sales of $1,300 per square foot, double the supermarket industry average.

What's your power source for bonding with customers?

Do you regularly connect with customers as they experience your products and services? Are you eating your food, wearing your clothes, and experiencing the same service you deliver to customers?

Detachment and cynicism comes when customers are defined only by research and reports.

Decide to BELIEVE.

CustomInk Decided
to Put Uncensored Customer Reviews on Their Home Page.

INTENT: Earn New Customers Through Past Performance.

CustomInk prints T-shirts for well over 100,000 groups and families per year. Each order is assigned a designer who personally reviews and inspects each shirt, because, let's face it, there's nothing worse than having your typing error printed on 1,000 T-shirts. For example, if you accidentally mistype the word "annual" as "anual" in your T-shirt design, someone at CustomInk who has reviewed your design will catch that typo for you, sparing the obvious pain and suffering you would have otherwise felt when you opened the box of 1,000 T-shirts for your "Anual Fun Run." But CustomInk doesn't want potential customers to take *their* word for the fact that they deliver this level of service—they want their *customers* to speak for them. So whatever a customer types in as his or her post-purchase online feedback appears word-for-word on the front page of CustomInk's Web site. And, in this case, to show the authenticity of the comments, customers' typos stay.

MOTIVATION: Customers Should Be Completely Informed.

Founder Marc Katz said, "We thought about cleaning customers' reviews and making them more like testimonials, but we decided that doesn't mean anything to the customer. Any company can pick a few great reviews. It's the fact that we leave these uncensored and show all of them. It's the 1 in a 100 few unhappy comments that show these are real." So CustomInk puts its money where their customers' mouths are. Customers tell other customers if they believe CustomInk is the place to trust for T-shirts for their charity event, or the T-shirts that their grandpa and entire family will wear at his 100th birthday party.

IMPACT: Revenue Quadrupled from 2004 to 2008. Customer Feedback Fuels Company Growth.

CustomInk believes and trusts customers to speak for the company. This brave decision to "bare" customer feedback has fueled significant double-digit growth every year since their inception. The company has quadrupled in revenue from $13.5 million in 2004 to $60 million in revenue in 2008. And this growth is largely organic, driven by customer love, and with no backing of venture capital. For its 200 employees, living up to customer accolades energizes them; people want to be part of a company that believes its customers. Consider giving your customers a forum to connect and convince one another to become your customers. It does take some daring, and trust in your customers' words. But it is a powerful way to engage your company in customer feedback and to drive accountability in resolving the issues that customers bring up.

Do You
DARE
to Bare

What Your Customers Share?

*Do you trust current customers
to guide future customers?*

Do you censor customer reviews?

*Do you believe in the truth of
your customers' words?*

Decide to BELIEVE.

Wegmans Food Markets Decided
No Customer Is Allowed to Leave Unhappy.

DECISION INTENT: Free Employees to Do What's Right for Customers.

Wegmans Food Markets is a privately held grocery store chain with 37,000 employees. The company generated an estimated $4.5 billion in revenue in 2007. What fuels Wegmans's growth are passion, training, and trust. In traditional retailing, customer experiences can become stilted when the frontline staff has a list of "do's" and "don'ts" regarding how far they can go to serve their customers. Wegmans wanted to eliminate the behind-the-scenes rules and the required permission from managers usually necessary in retail. So the company decided to let employees make their own decisions no matter what customer situation they encounter. At Wegmans there is no rule book. There is simply this: no customer is allowed to leave unhappy.

MOTIVATION: A Trained, Trusted Employee Will Do the Right Thing.

CEO Danny Wegman believes in giving employees extensive training and experience to garner an understanding of the product and service experiences they are trusted to deliver. Wegmans invests over 40 hours per year on training to back up people's natural instincts to do the right thing with the necessary skills to help them take action. This allows Wegmans to free themselves of management oversight. Instead, they simply trust in the decision making of the people on the floor working with customers. That could mean deciding to give away a birthday cake to a customer whose order was accidentally misscheduled. Or cooking a turkey for a frazzled hostess who bought a turkey too large for her oven.

IMPACT: Annual Employee Turnover Is 7 Percent; Average for Grocery Stores is 19 Percent.

By giving staff control over their own decisions and believing in them, Wegmans can deliver what Danny Wegman calls "telepathic levels of service." This makes employees want to stay. The low turnover of 7 percent versus 19 percent for comparably-sized grocery store chains enables Wegmans to redirect the money it would have spent on constant recruiting to the constant development of their folks. And with that, profitability has followed. Wegmans's operating margins are estimated at 7.5 percent—double that of its competitors. And its sales per square foot are 50 percent higher than the industry average. By throwing away the rule book, Wegmans prospers both financially and in the spirit of the people who work in its stores. Whether they're putting away cans of garbanzo beans or sweeping the floor, everyone there knows that their decisions with customers stick. What portion of your rule book can you throw away?

Is Your Trusting "Cup"

Half Full or Half Empty?

Do you trust the majority of employees to do the right thing?

Or do you manage to the minority?

Decide to BELIEVE.

Chick-fil-A Decided
to Hire for Life.

DECISION INTENT: Hire People with a Track Record of Successful Relationships.

Chick-fil-A is a privately held restaurant chain famous for its chicken sandwich menu. Their 1,422 franchised stores in the United States are so beloved that people camp out prior to an opening so they can be the first to bite into the warm bun with the juicy chicken inside. President Dan Cathy often joins them during these overnight hurrahs—to partake in the fun, to thank the customers, and to spur on the people toiling inside making those sandwiches. And that is the secret sauce for Chick-fil-A . . . it's those people inside and how they are selected. At Chick-fil-A, they select for the long term. The company screens for the kinds of activities and relationships that candidates have sustained over a period of time. This gives an indication of their future relationships with others in the stores and with customers.

MOTIVATION: People with Successful Relationships Fit the Culture and Stay.

Chick-fil-A sees their role as providing well-being along with a paycheck to the many young people who come onboard as teens. Chick-fil-A strives to provide an environment where employees can grow in their careers as they grow in life. They base selection on what they call the "three C's": Competence is the business acumen and the skills that they have. Character: their values. Last but not least is Chemistry, their "likability." Is this someone we would want our own sons or daughters to work for? Someone has said that it is easier getting a job with the CIA than it is with CFA. "We try to live up to that reputation," Cathy says. Chick-fil-A selects people who already have a history of successful relationships.

IMPACT: Sustainability of Chick-fil-A: Operator Turnover Is Only 5 Percent.

Hiring for life may sound a bit extreme, but for Chick-fil-A, this commitment is the secret behind its growth strategy. The sustainability of that chicken sandwich and store experience is dependent on operators who stay and grow their customer relationships and markets. So Chick-fil-A spends an extensive amount of time getting to know the values and habits of candidates so they can entrust their franchisees for life. This approach contributes to the stability of the operation of their stores and company growth. Chick-fil-A sales have almost quadrupled over the past decade. In 2008 system-wide sales were reported at $2.96 billion. Sales increased 12 percent over 2007 and same-store sales rose 4.6 percent. The company added 83 stores, ending 2008 with 1,422 outlets. Is your selection process rigorous enough to make sure you are bringing in partners who share your values?

Are you Hiring **Partners?**

or Filling **Positions?**

Do you select for lifelong values?
Are the people who enter your business
today people you want to become a part
of the story of your business?

Decide to BELIEVE.

Harley-Davidson Decided
to Partner with Unions and Employees.

DECISION INTENT: Partner for Sustainable Growth.

In the mid-1990s the senior management of Harley-Davidson and the presidents of two international unions, the International Association of Machinists (IAM) and the Paper, Allied-industrial, Chemical, and Energy Workers (PACE), decided to work together to establish a mutually beneficial partnership. They wanted to fundamentally change how they did business to increase product quality through partnership. And they wanted to make Harley-Davidson a better place to work. This landmark decision to create union and employer partnerships created a new shared leadership between the business and union leaders and enabled Harley-Davidson to innovate as demand increased for their vehicles.

MOTIVATION: Trust Breeds Accountability and Passion.

To increase output within the existing Harley-Davidson U.S. factories and build a new factory to keep up with demand, Harley-Davidson and IAM/PACE union leadership put their new partnership to the test. Traditionally, union and nonunion workers did not mix, but Harley-Davidson decided to demolish that barrier in order to achieve better product quality and to invigorate the workforce. Teams of never before paired union and nonunion members, many of whom were line workers, came together for the building of a plant in Texas. These teams chose the plant location and were involved for the first time in the hiring process. As a result of partnership actions, efficiency increased and the need for management oversight decreased.

IMPACT: Harley-Davidson Builds Lifelong Partnerships.

Jeffrey Bleustein, former Harley-Davidson chairman and CEO, said, "Through partnering, we've created an environment where all employees are valued and expected to make good decisions to benefit the enterprise." That decision defines the spirit of all of Harley-Davidson's partnerships. For example, strong dealer partnerships make it very challenging for competitors to take market share from them. Today, Harley-Davidson controls more than 49 percent of the annual market share of heavyweight motorcycles in the United States and more than 30 percent worldwide. When asked through surveys, over 80 percent of Harley riders regularly validate that yes, of course, their next motorcycle will be a Harley-Davidson. Do you involve employees in planning their own destiny? How do you embrace your partners? Are you nurturing a company of contributors?

Who Has a Seat at Your Table?

Do you honor genuine partnership and believe in its power?

Are you nurturing a company of contributors?

Decide to BELIEVE.

What Do Customers and Employees Say About Your Ability to Believe?

BELIEVING, the act of honoring and trusting is a unique and special characteristic that sets beloved companies apart. It makes them human. And it bonds people to them.

Your decisions grounded in belief prove how much you honor customers and employees. They say how fearless you are in suspending cynicism. They indicate whether you nurture people and relationships to their full potential. What you decide to believe defines the spirit inside your organization. And it sets the tone for your interactions with customers. Search within your organization for these indicators of your ability to believe:

- How much trust exists in the front line to make decisions for customers?
- Are all the rules necessary?
- Is your selection process rigorous enough to allow you the freedom to trust the people you hire?
- Does your company have an intrinsic trusting relationship with customers?

Trusting your employees and customers goes beyond blind belief. Belief includes the selection and preparation of employees so they can do their best work. Belief includes building a reciprocal relationship of trust with customers, which may mean sharing information that would benefit customers even if it's information you've feared to share in the past. It means setting up customers for success and prosperity. It means showing customers the rule book and getting rid of stupid rules that aren't necessary in a relationship based on belief. The story of the companies who believe is about how great it feels to come in contact with them. And about how that sets the company and its people apart. Do you believe?

Do You Believe...

In the good judgment of the people you hire?

That trust is reciprocated by customers?

In the truth of your customers' words?

That trusted and prepared employees grow the business?

In more trust than rules. In more training than policies?

How would customers describe your trust in them?

Would employees say you honor them?

What's Your Story:
How you BELIEVE.

If you create an environment where the people truly participate, you don't need control. They know what needs to be done and they do it. And the more that people will devote themselves to your cause on a voluntary basis, a willing basis, the fewer hierarchies and control mechanisms you need.

—Herb Kelleher, founder,
Southwest Airlines

For a tool kit on how to use these questions to improve your business go to www.customerbliss.com.

3

Decide with CLARITY *of* PURPOSE

Many people have a wrong idea of what
constitutes true happiness. It is not attained
through self-gratification, but through fidelity
to a worthy purpose.

—HELEN KELLER

The companies beloved by their customers, those that are true and authentic, work hard every day to resist the pull of "normal" business practices to create a powerful human connection with their customers. They are able to do this because they have something which binds everyone together, moving them toward a common goal: clarity of purpose.

Beloved companies take the time to be clear about what their unique promise is for their customers' lives. They use this clarity when they make decisions so they align to this purpose, to this promise. Clarity of purpose guides choices and unites the organization. It elevates people's work from executing tasks to delivering experiences customers will want to repeat and tell others about.

In the technology sector, Apple's clarity for creating its in-store experience has built a cult following. Someone you know has probably stood in line to get a newly released product or bellied up to their Genius Bar. Trader Joe's, a grocery store so clearly focused on personal interaction with customers, obsessed over the decision to buy scanning equipment. They worried that the scanning equipment's "pinging" sound would get in the way of their employees' chatty conversations with customers. An e-commerce site, Newegg.com, banned pop-up ads after checkout. They won't abdicate their well-orchestrated customer experience and final memory to a third-party partner's pop-up ad, even though pop-up ads bring in extra revenue.

Apple stores wouldn't have become the gathering place they are today without the time, angst, and thought that went into deciding

what those stores would and *would not* be. Apple decided its store would
be a gathering place, a place to experience its products and to meet
other Apple enthusiasts. They decided it would not be a traditional
boxed-software store. That one decision cleared the way for the thousands that followed that eventually turned Apple Stores into the Mecca
they are to their fans. Trader Joe's could not remain the wildly prosperous grocery store destination for its impassioned customers
without clarity of purpose. Trader Joe's was clear from the start that
their store experience be remembered for its warm and personal
interactions with everyone in the store, from people stocking merchandise to people checking out customers. Because of that clarity,
anything that potentially threatened the ability to carry out those
conversations was scrutinzed. For most e-commerce sites, pop-up ads
after checkout are considered a smart way to drive additional revenue.
Newegg.com said, "No, that's not what our experience is all about."
They couldn't have made that decision without clarity of purpose.

Beloved Companies Decide with Clarity of Purpose.

"Our iron-clad integrity and clarity guides the direction
of our decisions."

At Genentech, one of the world's fastest-growing and admired bio-
tech companies, clarity of purpose fuels its growth. The personal
knowledge of patients, and the details of the lives they are saving,
motivates employees to make the right decisions for the customers
they serve. It elevates their decisions from science . . . to saving lives.

Walk in the doors of Genentech's offices and there is no mistaking
this company's purpose. Ahead of you on the wall are the faces of
Susan, Paulo, Gloria, Kris, and many others. Welcome to Genentech.
"In Business for Life." Susan, Paulo, Gloria, and Kris are the patients—
and improving their lives and saving them compel the people who
work there to be passionate about what they do. The faces connect
their work to the human beings they ultimately serve. Their job is to
keep people alive. The obsession for being "in business for life" is
owned by everyone there—from the company's scientists to Cynthia

Wong in sales. Her reason for being part of Genentech? She talks about a breast cancer patient with two little girls. "She wants to see them in braces. She wants to be there when they pick out their prom dresses," Wong explained. Genentech employees are there to make sure those days come.

Each beloved company makes key decisions to mark its place in the universe with customers. Beloved companies begin with a notion, an idea fueled by passion about their greater purpose for improving customers' lives. It doesn't matter if they are selling electronics or food, or saving lives; conviction helps them stay the course. Even in the face of sacrifice and, yes, sometimes pain, beloved companies press on for customers. They persevere until they get it right.

One of the most heralded and humane responses to a corporate crisis might not have occurred if Johnson & Johnson's clarity of purpose hadn't been challenged and recommitted to just three years prior to the infamous event in which seven consumers in the Chicago area died

"Beloved companies begin with a notion, an idea fueled by passion, about their greater purpose."

from Tylenol capsules that had been tampered with and laced with cyanide. James Burke was CEO of Johnson & Johnson in 1982 when the tragedy struck, and he and his team responded by taking swift accountability, removing over $100 million of Tylenol products from stores, and quickly warning consumers. Even though Johnson & Johnson was not culpable in the tampering, it did not waste precious time in accusations and placing blame as the event unfolded. The primary decision made was "How do we protect the people?" Their decisions in response to this event saved countless lives and placed Johnson & Johnson in high esteem around the world.

An uncomfortable meeting of Burke and his leadership team three years earlier enabled the team to make such decisions swiftly and without hesitation or debate. This critical meeting was brought on by a major concern of Burke's that the Johnson & Johnson credo was no longer being considered as a relevant guide for decision making in running the company.

The company's businesses were operationally efficient, but he worried that core business decisions weren't actively considering the commitment in the credo penned by the company founders—which included "having a higher duty to mothers and all others who use our products." Burke is quoted as having said to his leadership team: "Here's the credo. If we're not going to live by it, let's tear it off the wall."

Burke's challenge prompted an entire afternoon of conversation in that conference room, and duplicate conversations around the world within all of Johnson & Johnson's businesses. He and his leaders challenged themselves and their decision making. They regrounded themselves in the meaning of their credo and how it needed to be translated into everyday decisions and actions. Consequently, when the Tylenol tragedy occurred, there was no question about how they would react; there was no debate. Clarity of purpose and living the credo paved the way for the decisions they made to clear shelves around the world of Tylenol products and to immediately lead the charge to ensure that no additional lives were lost.

What's Your Promise?
Does It Live Consistently Across Your Company?

Clarity of purpose extends well beyond the boardrooms of beloved companies. It unleashes the organization's imagination to make decisions guided by its promise. It's no wonder that companies with clarity of purpose have the most loyal and engaged employees. The opportunity to deliver to a clear purpose elevates day-to-day tasks, giving work direction and joy.

Internet clothing and shoe retailer Zappos.com earns 75 percent of their daily orders from repeat customers. Clarity of purpose fuels its customer devotion. Zappos wants to be known as a service company that happens to sell shoes, handbags, and an expanding array of products in the future. The lens through which the company makes decisions is service. This clarity frees everyone there to live the "Golden Rule" in the way they work.

One decision Zappos acts on every day is helping customers find a pair of shoes, even a pair they don't stock. Customer Loyalty Reps who take customer calls are encouraged to know competitors' Web sites for one simple purpose: service. If a customer calls Zappos for a shoe it doesn't have, their Reps will search the Internet to help the customer find it. Customers are continuously amazed, delighted, and dazzled by this act of genuine customer care.

> "Clarity of purpose . . .
> unleashes the organization's
> imagination to make decisions
> guided by its promise."

Zappos' clarity of purpose—that doing the right thing for the customer is ultimately the right thing for the business—transcends any short-term gain it might get by pushing the customer toward another shoe they have in stock. Clarity for being a service business *first* gives Customer Loyalty Reps energy and a compass for decision making. And it gives them the joy of delivering Zappos' version of the "Miracle on 34th Street." You may remember that in the movie *Miracle on 34th Street*, a Macy's-employed department store Santa joyfully sends customers to competitors when the store didn't stock what they wanted, making Macy's the "winner" of the Christmas season. In this single, simple decision, Zappos wins over customers' hearts. It is this type of gesture that makes customers love them. They are loved for being the kind of people who send a customer to the competition because it's the right thing to do.

> "They are loved for being
> the kind of people who
> send a customer to the
> competition because it's
> the right thing to do."

Every type of business prospers when clarity of purpose steers decision making. People across your company live up to the promises you make. Customers become emotionally connected with you and want others to experience what you deliver. Their stories of your service, experience, and people become the folklore that defines you. And customers become your sales force, telling your story to everyone they know, fueling your growth.

Southwest Airlines builds memories that pull customers back not just for the plane ride but for how they feel throughout the experience. Their clarity of purpose for how they run their business, as a low-cost carrier with heart and personality, comes through in their customers' own words. No marketing material required, their passengers are Southwest Airlines' sales force. Customers describe Southwest's service, of course, but also the people—the bearers of the human and emotional connection that exists between Southwest and its customers. Here are just a couple from Yelp.com:

- "The flight attendants on Southwest are a treat—they never seem bitter about their job and always provide comedic entertainment."
- "People complain about the open seating, but I love it. First come, first serve, just like everything else in life. If you grew up in a big family you would understand this concept."

Memory Creation Is the Currency of Your Brand. Are You Leaving Customer Memories to Chance?

Clarity of purpose means having a definition of what experiences you will deliver. It means knowing what memory you want customers to have and making the decisions to prepare your people and your operation to deliver it. Memory creation—creating indelible remembrances of the customer experience—is the currency of your brand. Beloved companies don't leave these memories to chance.

The difference between beloved companies and others is that their clarity of purpose gives them a lens to go beyond merely executing tasks to delivering points of contact that connect with their customer's lives. Clarity of purpose expands the definition of work—from making drugs to saving lives, from selling homes to delivering the American Dream. Companies with clarity of purpose can turn task-oriented decisions into choices that lift them up and differentiate them. In the beloved companies:

- Decisions connect, guided by the clarity of a common purpose.
- Clarity of purpose elevates the work of everyone in the organization.

Following is a set of decisions to help you learn what level of clarity guides your decisions, so you can gain an understanding of how many different versions of the story of your experience are being told. Companies in all industries prosper when they have clarity of purpose and use it to steer direction and choices.

The Decision Is Yours.

Apple Decided
to Open a Bar in Their Stores.

DECISION INTENT: Dispense Technology Advice in a Warm and Engaging Manner.

When Apple was planning its stores, they were envisioned as a place where people would congregate to experience the products and each other. Ron Johnson, senior vice president of retail, described his vision: "I imagined it as a store for everyone, a place that would be welcoming to all ages and where people could feel they truly belonged." Johnson's past visits to the Ritz-Carlton and Four Seasons hotel bars, in particular, struck a nerve while he was envisioning the store experience, because they had a sense of community, a warm engaging environment. He was inspired to replicate that same feeling in the Apple Stores. Starting with that notion, Johnson created Apple's Genius Bars. Apple put their version of a bar in the stores . . . one that dispensed advice instead of alcohol.

MOTIVATION: Make Apple Stores a Destination, a Community.

The clarity that guided this one decision, to make the stores a place of community and belonging, triggered decisions that have made Apple Stores the destinations they have become today. Why can anyone use the bathrooms in Apple Stores? To establish community and belonging. Why does Apple hire people of all ages and backgrounds? To build community and belonging. Why did they put in the Genius Bars? To build community and belonging. When there is a clear and simple purpose that shapes and guides actions, decisions of the organization connect. Clarity has made the Apple Store a beloved destination.

IMPACT: Apple's Stores Became the Fastest Retailer to Reach $1 Billion in Annual Revenues.

What sets companies that customers love apart from the others is that they imagine the experience first. Then—and only then—can they deliver it. Apple imagined people clustered around a bar in a place buzzing with energy and warmth. Apple built it and people came. Apple's stores were the fastest retailer to ever reach $1 billion in annual revenues, which was achieved in just three years. During 2007, 102.4 million people were welcomed into those stores and in fiscal 2008 Apple Retail Stores revenue grew to $6.3 billion. Clarity of purpose also creates and keeps engaged employees serving customers. Of Apple's 16,000 retail employees, 20 percent per year leave, compared to 50 percent on average for the retail industry. This is due in large part because these folks are a part of delivering an experience that is clear to them and that they believe in. This clarity begins at home—inside the four walls of your company. Walk your halls and ask ten people to define your higher purpose with customers. What kinds of answers would you get?

What Defines
Your
Experience?

Would 10 random people in your company give the same definition for your customer experience?

If not,
imagine
what you're
delivering.

Decide with CLARITY.

Zappos.com Decided
to Offer People $2,000 to Leave.

DECISION INTENT: Sustain Zappos's Culture While Growing Rapidly.

Internet clothing and shoe retailer Zappos.com reached over $1 billion in gross merchandise sales in 2008. Zappos's growth is powered by service and a whimsical culture. Essential to this growth is attracting people to work at Zappos who find it natural, according to one of their core values, to be "a little weird at times." Zappos conducts a rigorous interview process which includes an initial culture interview, followed by many conversations throughout the company to find just the right people who will fit in and, most important, feel at home in the Zappos culture. And while they do their best to get to know candidates during the interview process, once someone is invited inside, Zappos continues their quest to make sure that there's a match between candidate and company. Offering new hires $2,000 to leave if they don't fit the culture is Zappos's litmus test to ensure that, well, the shoe fits.

MOTIVATION: Only the Most Passionate Employees Should Stick Around.

Zappos doesn't want anybody sticking around who sees their role with them as just a job. They want people with passion who see Zappos as an avocation rather than work, one which you just happen to get paid for. Zappos sees what they do as a quest to make the world a better place for customers, and they want to hire people who feel that way too. So the company makes several offers during the four-week new-hire training period to say, "Are you sure?" "Is this the place where you feel at home?" And in true Zappos style, if someone does decide that the shoe doesn't fit, the company makes sure that they're paid for their time, that they leave with dignity, and that their decision is honored. Tony Hsieh, Zappos's CEO, says, "We want people who are eager to live the Zappos lifestyle and promote the Zappos culture—not a typical nine-to-five office employee."

IMPACT: Fewer than 1 Percent Take Zappos Up on the Offer to Depart.

In 2008, less than 1 percent of new hires took Zappos up on their offer. That means that those who stay are committed and passionate. As a result of their interviewing and training process, Zappos is an electric place, filled with people who want to be there. It's filled with people who are encouraged to bring out their inner whimsy. The IT crowd holds parades in which they dress as bugs because their quest is to stamp out computer bugs. Where "Zapponians" work is filled with karaoke music at lunchtime and people who couldn't imagine being anywhere else or doing any other thing. Selling to a fiercely loyal customer base of over 10 million paying customers, the company can boast that on any given day approximately 75 percent of Zappos's sales are to repeat customers.

Do You Hire People Who Fit The Soul Of Your Company?

Do You Encourage Those Who Don't To Leave?

If you don't, everything you're building is on shaky ground. Customer interactions will always vary between great experiences delivered by passionate people and mediocre ones delivered by the rest. Beloved companies are filled with people who love what they do.

Decide with CLARITY.

Zane's Cycles Decided to Guarantee the Entire Customer Experience.

DECISION INTENT: Guarantee Happiness. Remove Price and Worry from Buying Decisions.

Most guarantees put the monkey on the customer's back to manage a countdown clock on product happiness. They put a limit on the time customers have to return a product after its purchase. That enforced timeline creates a transaction-based relationship with customers, as they measure happiness one purchase at a time. Zane's decided to guarantee the happiness of the customer relationship instead. They threw out the clock. The Zane's guarantee says: "We are going to live up to our promises, no matter what the timing, no matter what the product or service."

MOTIVATION: Eliminate Any Reason for Not Considering Zane's.

Founder Chris Zane knows that each customer who walks through its door brings $12,500, on average, to the business over the lifetime of the relationship. The intention behind this guarantee is to eliminate any reason for not considering Zane's Cycles and earning that new customer. So Zane's guarantee includes everything: lifetime free service, a 90-day price guarantee, a lifetime parts warranty. With these promises, Zane's says to customers: "Why worry about price when our price is guaranteed? We will live up to our promise." And this promise guides decision making throughout

the lifetime of every Zane's customer. For example, a customer who wants to return a $500 item is gladly given the refund. It is not worth jeopardizing the future value of that relationship. Zane's employees embrace that: it's not $500 at risk, it's a $12,500 customer.

IMPACT: Zane's Cycles Sells $13 Million Worth of Bikes and Parts with a Single Store.

Companies who understand their customers' lives grow their business, and earn the right to customers telling their story to everyone they know. Zane's earns the right to their customers' stories with their decision to guarantee bicycle ownership. In a world where there is so little that customers can count on, this promise delivers "wow" in a world of customer service vanilla. And it fuels Zane's growth. By taking away any fear in buying, Zane's customers are less prone to negotiating a bike's price, because in the long term, they know they'll be covered by the Zane's guarantee. Zane's can maintain its margins because price is never the determining factor in a customer decision. Customers know that "if I buy it and I don't like it, I can bring it back." Zane's customers look forward to the ownership experience—also guaranteed. What part of your experience can you guarantee? How do you make sure your customers sleep well at night, knowing you've got them covered?

Does Your *Experience* Have an *Expiration Date?*

Do your service offerings put the monkey on customers' backs to keep track of when and how they can get help from you, redeem points, or take advantage of your warranty?

What part of your experience can you guarantee to give your customers trouble-free peace of mind?

Decide with CLARITY.

Umpqua Bank Decided to Get Rid of the Ropes.

DECISION INTENT: Elevate Banking from Chore to Great Experience.

We've all stood in that bank line. Walking between two ropes which force us into a single-file lane, we shuffle slowly, waiting our turn, with nothing to do but watch the person at the counter, look at our watches, and wait for it all to be over. And if there's a request that the teller can't handle, there's another line, and more shuffling. Well, they got rid of those ropes and the lines at Umpqua Bank. As part of Umpqua's metamorphosis from "bank" to "store," led by CEO Ray Davis, they shed the ropes and most standard banking practices to get rid of the feeling that banking was a chore.

MOTIVATION: Compel Customers to Want to Return.

Umpqua Bank has a quirky, light-hearted nature for a financial services company, perhaps because they started with the simple goal to help loggers and farmers with their banking. But despite their heartfelt purpose of being "the loggers' bank," customer experiences prior to 1994 were not consistently strong. Service levels varied from one day to the next, from one teller to the next. I call this "biorhythmic" service, in which customer experiences vary by service provider and by what kind of day he or she is having. Observing Umpqua's lack of a clear customer-service approach, CEO Ray Davis decided to make a change. In a move away from traditional banking, he renamed Umpqua locations "stores." In redesigned "stores," "shoppers" could browse products and services, stay as long as they wanted, sit a spell with their legs up on a comfy chair, and sip a cup of coffee. And when they were ready, they could tap an Umpqua associate to help them with their banking needs. All without the red ropes. At Umpqua, customers are not herded into a line for service, and they don't have to stand in separate lines to get different services. Dedicated associates assist each customer from start to finish

IMPACT: Customers Stay and Put Their Feet Up at Umpqua Bank.

"Umpqua Bank is part Internet café, part community center, and part bank. The coffee's good and it's not a bad place to sit and read a book." By shedding old industry practices and warming up and humanizing the experience of banking, Umpqua draws customers to them. Through transforming banking into an enjoyable shopping experience, its original five branches from 1994 are now part of a 148-bank network across two states with $8.6 billion in assets (up 3.6 percent from $8.3 billion in 2007). Do you have your own version of banking lines that you make customers shuffle through to get help from you? Can you find a way to get rid of your version of the "red ropes"?

If you shed standard industry practices…

What could you *become*?

Decide with CLARITY.

Griffin Hospital Decided
on Music in the Parking Lot and a Piano in the Lobby.

DECISION INTENT: A Griffin Hospital Visit Should Be Uplifting, Not Avoided.

In chapter 1, you were introduced to Griffin Hospital, a local Connecticut hospital that has earned extreme customer loyalty. What I didn't tell you earlier is that back in 1982, Griffin Hospital was very far from extreme loyalty. At that time, one-third of the local community named Griffin as the hospital they would avoid if they could. That rude awakening pushed Griffin to rethink their purpose and literally everything they did.

MOTIVATION: Make Griffin the Hospital of Choice in the Community.

Being told that it was avoided whenever possible pushed Griffin to rethink the purpose for their hospital, physicians, and caregivers. Their goal was to go from being the hospital to avoid to being the hospital of choice in the community. Griffin knew that if "choice" was the goal, then they had to readjust their purpose; they needed to move from being healthcare providers to becoming service providers. Griffin had to stop executing required tasks and determine what *experience* they would deliver, what patient and family emotions were involved. What they found was that the emotional journey of going to the hospital begins in the parking lot. So Griffin provides free valet parking and concierge services. Music in the parking lot and lobby welcomes

visitors and takes away the sterile "hospital" feeling. Says Bill Powanda, Griffin Hospital vice president, "It doesn't matter if you have the shortest Emergency Department wait times around and deliver the greatest care in the nation; if parking is a nightmare, your patients won't be completely satisfied."

IMPACT: Griffin Hospital's Growth Is Three Times the Rate of Other Connecticut Hospitals.

Understanding the customer emotions involved in "coming and going" from a hospital visit prompted actions that made Griffin stand out. Those bookend experiences are part of the magnet that pulls people back to Griffin. No longer considered the "black sheep" hospital of the community, Griffin's growth rate is three times the average for hospitals in the state. Inpatient admissions grew 31 percent from 1998 to 2007, compared with a state average growth rate of 5.7 percent. And outpatient services grew 70 percent. Not only have they become the choice of their community, but for surrounding communities as well. One-third of Griffin Hospital's customers come from outside of the community it serves. Ten percent of administrators of U.S. hospitals want to visit Griffin Hospital to learn from them. Do you think about how you punctuate your moments of connection with customers? First impressions last the longest. Is yours purposeful? Does it create the ideal first opinion of you?

What are your customer experience bookends?

Do you have a purposeful beginning and ending to moments of customer contact?

Are you creating memories?

Or executing tasks?

Decide with CLARITY.

LUSH Cosmetics Decided
to Retire 100 Products per Year.

DECISION INTENT: Keep LUSH Customers Engaged and Passionate.

There's a rule of thumb at LUSH cosmetics, and that's to fearlessly retire one-third of the product line every year. Change is the magic behind the suds at LUSH. Rather than waiting for customers to tire of products, LUSH imposes a rigorous process to get rid of the old to make way for the new. It is what keeps LUSH fresh, and it is what keeps pulling customers back. LUSH grows because customers fuel its growth. Remember when you were a kid and couldn't walk by a candy store without going in, because of the lure and the scent of the candy? That's how LUSH lures people into their stores. It's hard to walk by without going in to see what's new, and it's hard to walk out of a LUSH store without a bag full of its fresh cosmetics.

MOTIVATION: Offer the Freshest Products in the History of Cosmetics.

"If anything, as businesses mature, they get more dull," says founder Mark Constantine. A major product development guru in his previous life at The Body Shop, Constantine had developed products that, by the 1980s, made up about 80 percent of that chain's sales. As The Body Shop matured, Constantine felt the fizz leave the business, and so he departed with his concept of the "bath bomb" and eventually founded LUSH. Irreverently calling their bath bomb "A Giant Alka-Seltzer for Your Tub," LUSH has stayed true to its core of creating natural products with surprising ingredients and off-the-wall names. To stay constantly fresh, LUSH brings together an annual meeting of senior managers for what it calls the "mafia meeting" because they decide what products to *kill* during this meeting. Their goal is to offer "the freshest products in the history of cosmetics." The company is making it happen by not sitting still. "Innovate like mad, then start over again" is the mantra LUSH lives.

IMPACT: A New LUSH Store Can Break Even in as Little as Three Months.

Every day, LUSH sells nearly 60,000 bath bombs, the concoction that created the LUSH fan base. LUSH spends little on advertising (customers spread the word) and packaging (they use less material to stay green). Because of this combination of customers' word of mouth growing the business and LUSH's enviable low margins resulting from minimal advertising and packaging, a new LUSH store can break even in as little as three months. In fiscal year 2007, 462 LUSH stores in 46 countries had combined revenue of $292 million, up 28 percent over fiscal 2006. It rose to a reported $338.4 million in fiscal 2008. What do you do to stay fresh for your customers? As customers' needs change, do you commit to understanding what they need? What should you consider retiring? A service, a practice, a product?

How
Fresh
Are You?

Are you fearless in dismissing the old and bringing in the new?

How do you keep your customers enticed and interested?

Decide with CLARITY.

Trader Joe's Decided
That EVERYONE Wears Hawaiian Shirts.

DECISION INTENT: Keep Everyone Connected to Trader Joe's Purpose.

In the early 1970s, Trader Joe's founder Joe Coulombe, who owned a small chain of convenience stores in Los Angeles, began struggling from the success of his newest competitor: 7-Eleven. Coulombe began to lure customers with what were then considered specialty foods, such as brie cheese, Dijon mustard, and wild rice. Inspired by the lure of these new "exotic" foods, his love of travel, a book he was reading called *Trader Horn*, and a trip to the Caribbean, Coulombe created the recipe for Trader Joe's grocery stores. Wanting customers to feel they were going on an excursion for food, he decked out his stores with rustic and nautical décor. (He named store managers "captains," "assistant managers," first mates) and dressed employees in Hawaiian shirts. Coulombe then began creating products to take customers' taste buds on a journey around the world.

MOTIVATION: Make Sure the Trader Joe's Vibe Stays Alive.

Donning that Hawaiian shirt puts Trader Joe's employees into character, reminding them that their job is to transport customers to a relaxing and lighthearted experience in the stores and with their products. Clarity and consistency at Trader Joe's—all the way down to those shirts—keeps them hiring and retaining people who find it part of their natural DNA to deliver a laid-back island vibe and a fulfilling shopping experience. Trader Joe's describes itself as "traders on the culinary seas, searching the world over for cool items to bring home to our customers." That means that everyone's a part of the journey, from crew members in the stores to the CEO.

IMPACT: Employee Turnover at Trader Joe's Is Only 4 Percent.

Trader Joe's is so emphatic about building a culture consistent with the fun of wearing that shirt that former CEO John Shields would tell new crew members that if they were not having fun at the end of their first 30 days to please resign. They don't want anyone to stay who can't "own" the vibe of the personal, lighthearted, and happy service you'd get at a roadside stand for juice in the Caribbean. For example, a June 28, 2008, blogger explained how the person bagging her groceries noticed that a package of salmon wasn't sealed correctly, so he swiftly sprinted to get her a sealed replacement. This is the Trader Joe's vibe; the automatic sprint to get some new fish and a smile as an extra, second piece is tossed into the cart. ("No worries, be happy.") Delivering on it attracts and keeps its valuable workforce. Voluntary employee turnover is only 4 percent. What can you do to remind employees of the vibe of your company? More important, do you *have* a vibe?

What's
Your
Vibe?

*Do you take yourself too seriously?
The beloved companies all laugh at
themselves at times. And they have
a certain personality that marks
them in their customers' memories.*

What's yours?

Decide with CLARITY.

IKEA Decided
to Design the Price Tag First.

DECISION INTENT: Innovation Guided by Function and Price.

IKEA is the "Popeye" of furniture stores. Committed and clear about their purpose, they are proud to say, "We are what we are." Their purpose is to "create a better everyday life for *many* people." IKEA wants to produce democratic design: products with flair at a price most people can afford. They know that even people on a limited budget want a beautiful home, a comfortable home, a place that feels like, well, home.

MOTIVATION: Draw Customers Who Count on IKEA to Fill Their Homes.

Beginning with the price tag first keeps IKEA aligned with their purpose. For example, the design process for a product called the Lillberg chair started with a target price of $139. Once the price was established, considerations for how customers would use the chair were factored into the design. Then material selection and form were defined, along with how the chair would be packaged. Packaging for IKEA is key, impacting both pricing and product design. In the case of this chair, the more chairs that can fit into a shipping container, the lower the price for the customer. In designing the Lillberg chair, after multiple trials and many months, a final tweak in the angle of the chair's arm decreased the packaging cost significantly and the target price

was met. Minimizing waste and creating functional yet desirable items to fill peoples' homes continues beyond product development into the IKEA store experience. The self-service environment lowers cost, passing the savings on to the customer. IKEA punctuates the store experience by placing an oasis for nourishment (a "do-it-yourself" cafeteria) smack-dab in the center of the store, serving Swedish meatballs, inexpensive hotdogs, and cinnamon rolls.

IMPACT: IKEA Was Named the Fastest-Growing Furniture Store in 2007.

By deciding to design the price tag first for their products, IKEA stays on course to what endears them to their customers. IKEA's sensible Scandinavian approach to design and pricing draws their core customers: young, just-starting-out singles and families who have much more energy than cash. The industry publication *Furniture Today* named IKEA the fastest-growing furniture store in 2007. The company moved from third to second place with $1.79 billion in furniture, bedding, and accessories sales. In fiscal 2008, 253 IKEA stores in 24 countries welcomed 565 million visitors. Do you have clarity like IKEA about your customers and what unique value you deliver to their lives? What do you always consider first in product and service development?

What pushes your "YES" button?

IKEA designs the price tag first.
It keeps them on course.

What steers your decisions?
What conditions must always
be met before you say **"yes"**?

Decide with CLARITY.

Newegg.com Decided Against Pop-Up Ads After Checkout.

DECISION INTENT: Always End Shopping on a Positive Note.
Newegg.com is the second-largest online-only retailer in the United States. They are like the "mother ship" to technology fanatics, carrying a dizzying level of inventory to ensure that customers can get what they want when they want it. At the core of Newegg.com's fast growth is their decision that they would grow through fanaticism for their customers and the experience they deliver to them. So once you've found the motherboard of your heart's desire or a flat-screen TV and proceed to checkout, Newegg.com makes sure that things stay between you and them. There are no pop-up ads from third-party vendors after you've finished your transaction, even though those ads would send more cash to Newegg.com. The company doesn't want to muck up the hard work it has put into its Web site and customer experience in the name of getting a few more dollars out of its shoppers

MOTIVATION: Keep Customers on the Web Site Longer and Compel Them to Return.
Clarity about how they want a customer experience to end led Newegg.com away from one that punctuates many Internet customer experiences. They wanted to become not only a place where customers go to buy, but also an important forum where technology fanatics go to chat with one another. This clarity for shoppers' experiences has paid off. Many customers stay on Newegg.com 20 minutes or longer— a testament to the fact that the site has become a destination, not just a place to buy something and depart. Newegg doesn't want to disturb the reverie of that experience with a pop-up ad. Not only do they want to deliver a closing memory, Newegg.com wants every part of their shopper's experience to be memorable and reliable.

IMPACT: Newegg.com Enjoys a Daily Average of 600,000 Visitors.
Newegg.com traded short-term financial gain from pop-up ads for long-term customer relationships. Still, they continue to be one of the fastest-growing retailers in their industry. In 2008, the company achieved the best year in their history. Closing with over $2 billion in sales. Newegg.com has grown to 11 million registered customers since their first order was placed in 2001 and enjoys approximately 600,000 average daily visitors to their Web site, who stay and shop four times longer than the industry average for online retailers. How can you take a cue from Newegg.com and own the closing memory for your customer? Do you have clarity on how you want the final moments of your customer interactions to play out?

Do you deliver
a closing
memory?

What's the last thing you want your customers to remember about you after they say "good-bye"?

Decide with CLARITY.

What's Your Story: How Clear Are You About Your Purpose?

Remember, the difference between beloved companies and others is that their clarity of purpose gives them a lens through which they make decisions that go beyond executing tasks to delivering points of contact that connect with their customers' lives. It frees them to come up with an inspired set of actions. Clarity of purpose expands the definition of work from making drugs to saving lives, from selling homes to delivering the American Dream. Companies with clarity of purpose can turn task-oriented decisions into choices that lift them up and differentiate them.

Clarity of purpose is your compass. With clarity of purpose, the decisions of your company connect. Across the organization, people work beyond executing a set of tasks. When there is clarity, your customer can easily tell the story of your company because your actions connect, all guided by a unifying purpose. You will be defined by what you do—more important, by *how* you do it.

Are customers clear about what you deliver and why it's different? Are your employees?

- If you ask ten people in your company what your purpose is, how many answers would you receive?
- Are customers telling your story?
- Are you selecting employees who are capable of delivering on your purpose?
- What steers decision making in one direction versus another?

With clarity of purpose, customers can easily tell the story of your company because your actions connect. Across the organization, people work toward delivering to a higher purpose rather than a set of tasks.

Do You Have Clarity About...

The memories you want to deliver?

The type of people who belong in your company?

How to steer decision making?

The experience you are all working toward?

Are your decisions directed toward executing tasks or achieving a purpose?

What's Your Story:
Clarity of PURPOSE.

For a tool kit on how to use these questions to improve your business, go to www.customerbliss.com.

4
Decide *to* BE REAL

**I think that somehow, we learn who we really are
and then live with that decision.**

—ELEANOR ROOSEVELT

One merchant I know, in a small Midwestern town, sold children's shoes. He gently steered mothers to the most appropriate, often less expensive shoe than those they had selected for their child. When these young mothers sometimes found themselves short on cash to pay for the shoes, the merchant said, without hesitation, "Take the shoes home and bring back the rest when you're back in town. Get those shoes on your little one's feet."

Alone in his store most of the time, he would fire up his hot plate to make a bit of lunch. Usually sausage, peppers and onions, and garlic. And the sound of olive oil popping and the aroma of garlic and sausage frying would float out to the front of the store. Customers who showed up around that time to buy their kids shoes (and the number always seemed to grow) would share in a bite, licking their fingers on their way out the door.

He "shoe'd" a generation of children, their children, and their children's children. And the warm habits of the merchant endeared him to his customers. When he retired, a line of people circled around the block to stop by to say that they'd miss him. That buying shoes would never be the same. The memory of his hands fitting the small feet of their children would last forever, and they could almost smell and taste the sausage every time they walked by the store. In his care of those tiny toes, with his quiet guiding hand, he earned a place in the hearts of a multitude of parents and children. My dad, selling those Buster Brown shoes, was the first one who taught me the importance of being real. Every pair of shoes he sold was delivered with a dose of heartfelt caring and often a mouthful of food. He didn't have a strategy or a plan for how he would connect with his customers. He did what came naturally. And he was loved for who he was.

Beloved Companies Decide to Be Real.

"We have a spirited soul, humanity in our touch, and personality that's all ours."

When a company strikes this kind of personal chord with customers, it's the anticipation of being in contact with people who act a certain way that pulls customers back into their fold. But can this personal and emotional connection exist beyond "mom and pop" neighborhood establishments to larger businesses? Can this type of humanity pass through the ranks of corporate structures and budget meetings and planning sessions? Can we bring our personal instincts to work with us and call on them in our business lives? Yes. The greatest leaders revel in being real. Their humanity and authenticity are what sets them apart. Their primary purpose is to nurture the organization to be able to live and work in this manner, where people can blend their personal instincts with their business decisions.

Do You Connect Your Personal "Self" with Your Business "Self"?

Indra Nooyi, CEO of PepsiCo, embraces who she is through how she leads. She is a disarmingly endearing combination of serious leader and "everymom." And she actively calls on both dimensions of her life in how she leads and gives people permission to lead and act. She was held to extremely high standards growing up. Her mother would pick, for example, one topic per evening on world or current events to discuss. Nooyi uses a similar tactic at work, pressing her teams to come up with solutions to problems, such as creating a lower cost alternative to palm oil. Colleagues say that Indra "brings her whole self" to work. Her delivery and how she talks about herself and her world are very real. She actively talks about being a mom, pushing her teams to create products that are healthy and easy to grab when it's your turn to provide the snacks at your child's school. Tough but real. Tough but human. Indra Nooyi teaches by example.

Colleen Barrett, President Emeritus of Southwest Airlines, says her company grows through heart, encouragement, and accountability. Southwest Airlines knew from the beginning that it needed to march to the beat of a different drummer to stand out in the crowded airline industry. "We wanted to be a household word," she told me, explaining Southwest's origins. "We wanted to become America's airline." In 1971 when Southwest initiated service, the "Americans" flying were mostly men. Southwest has never been afraid of putting its own "real" stamp on the flying experience. So while other stewardesses (they were not called flight attendants back then) wore conservative suits, Southwest stewardesses wore outfits that included hot pants and go-go boots to appeal to those passengers who were flying. "They ate up those hot pants and go-go boots!" Barrett said.

> **"Each beloved company makes key decisions to mark its place in the universe with customers."**

As Southwest expanded its service to a broader audience, the hot pants got the boot. Personality, compassion, customer service, and whimsy took their place. Southwest began bonding with customers, all customers, from its heart. Customers love Southwest for their candor and no-nonsense style when it comes to the business of running an airline. Customers are its biggest defenders and keepers of the Southwest Airlines way of doing business.

Barrett told me a story that proves this point. Herb Kelleher, Southwest Airline's founder, and she were in the Albuquerque, New Mexico, airport lounge area when a Southwest flight was boarding. Kelleher appeared to be just your average "Joe" waiting for his flight. As Barrett tells it, "An elderly woman went up to Herb and said, 'Young man, you better get your butt in gear—this airline goes when it says it is going to!'" She got a hug and a thank-you from both Barrett and Kelleher.

Thirty-seven years after Southwest began flying; they are thriving when other airlines are clinging to survival. Southwest has never purported to be all things to all people, but for those customers who gravitate to its brand of experience and humanity—a no-frills airline that will get you where you want to go but won't deliver food beyond peanuts, or attitude beyond warmth and sometimes good-natured sarcasm—the bond is strong.

Another company that revels in being real is LUSH cosmetics. Founder Mark Constantine keeps it real with thousands of self-proclaimed "Lushies" on its online forums who chat with Constantine and his staff. Here you see back-and-forth debate and straight talk usually reserved for friends. Customers often plead the case for products scheduled for extinction. LUSH lets people know ahead of time so they can stock up on their favorites headed for the chopping block. These exchanges set the tone for the honest, passionate, and straightforward relationship the rest of the company is encouraged to build with customers.

Likened in the media to Willy Wonka, Constantine orchestrates a cacophony of wild discovery techniques to find the scents (and textures) that will explode in the bath or soothe the skin, transporting LUSH customers to their quiet reverie. Some would say LUSH has drawn women back into the bath. LUSH has elevated the art of taking baths with the invention of the "bath bomb," calling it "a giant Alka-Seltzer for your tub." For the $7–$9 price of a bath bomb, they provide a bit of therapy for the soul. Laugh if you want—LUSH is laughing all the way to the bank. This unique, all-natural company, which hires people to crack open coconuts and peel mangoes to make its products, has created a legion of followers. LUSH Cosmetics has blossomed from one store in 1995 to more than 600 shops worldwide.

> "Beloved companies teach by example in the decisions they make, not by policy."

At Lands' End we had a folksy style that celebrated our Wisconsin roots. Customers connected with us, responding as if we were neighbors. So, true to our nature, in 1987, when we started the kids' business, we sent one of our native farm animals home to every customer to commemorate the occasion. The inside flaps of the shipping boxes were imprinted with the head and tail of a cow, a sheep, or a horse, so that the boxes could be transformed into an animal which kids could "ride" around the house for fun.

The point we were making was to symbolically stick our hand out of the box and say, "We know what it's like to have kids, and we have them too. Enjoy the clothes, and here's something for your little one to enjoy. Because, like you, we remember what fun playing with a box can be." We created new memories for a generation of parents who recalled playing with the boxes as much as they did the contents. We were able to take these steps because our motivation was to create an emotional connection. And that inspired us to go beyond the ordinary to the unexpected. In those early days, these uniquely Lands' End actions set us apart.

What sets beloved companies apart from the rest is how they get to these types of decisions in the first place. Beloved companies teach by example in the decisions they make, not by policy. They get past the hype and the packaging and focus on the moment of connection with the customer. They're the ones who dream up how to turn shipping boxes into farm animals, and then do the work to make it happen.

How Do You Decide to Be Real?

Companies that customers love work hard not to lose their personality—not in their products, not in their service, not in anything they do. They become beloved because of how they connect with customers in their lives. They relate personally with them. And their personalities come through during interaction with them.

Beloved companies may have quirky natures—but what beats beneath is a spirited soul. They stumble and fall from time to time, but are not timid about baring their foibles to customers. The genuine and authentically true companies are more important to customers than those that make false promises or the loud, trumped-up ones that don't deliver. Marketing ploys and offers won't make customers loyal or earn their trust. But being "real" and authentic will. Beloved companies establish lasting bonds with customers—by deciding to blend their personalities with their business decisions.

In the beloved companies:

- Leaders blend who they are as people with how they lead.
- Business decisions combine purpose and passion.
- Leaders give employees behaviors to model and *permission* to be "real."
- Relationships are between people who share the same values.

These attitudes and actions embody what is behind beloved companies. They take what informs their personal decisions with them into business. They let their roots influence decision making. Inside beloved companies, people call upon their personal experiences to inform their behavior. And they blend it with their business acumen to accomplish extraordinary outcomes.

Here is your set of decisions to help you evaluate how real and authentic you seem to customers by the business decisions you make. How do the actions that come from your decisions reveal the story of who you are as people and as an organization? Does your personal authenticity come through when you decide which direction to take your business?

The Decision Is Yours.

USAA Decided
That New Hires Should Eat Like Soldiers.

DECISION INTENT: Understand Customers to Serve Their Lives.

USAA (United Services Automobile Association) is a San Antonio company offering auto and home insurance to a customer base of military members and their families. While new hires are not required to be from the military, they must understand military life. So new USAA employees wear the military helmet and feel the weight of the backpack and flak vest as it is strapped to their backs. And they eat the same meals, the MREs—"meals ready to eat"—that soldiers eat in the field. They get to know the people behind the uniform by reading letters from soldiers and their families. As orientation ends, USAA's intent has been realized. They have made their customers' life a reality for their new recruits. And that sets the stage for how customers will be served.

MOTIVATION: Company Profitability Increases with Customer Growth.

USAA knows that an empathetic and caring workforce that understands the unique lives of their customer base is fundamental to their ongoing success and profitability. That means walking in their customers' shoes, literally. USAA calls their approach to connecting employees' lives with customers' lives "surround sound." Elizabeth D. Conklyn, USAA's executive vice president of people services, says, "We want to cover the light moments, the heart-wrenching moments, what it's like to be bored in the field." The company takes that understanding beyond orientation. For example; USAA call center reps are called "troops" and use military time on the job. And they commit to ongoing training with military precision and follow-through. In 2007, USAA put 12,400 "member service representatives" through 250,000 total hours of classes to reinforce basic training.

IMPACT: USAA Retained 98 Percent of Their Customers in 2008.

By walking in the shoes of its customers, USAA breaks down the impersonal barrier that often exists between companies and customers. As a result, USAA customers love and reward them with growth and validation; 98 percent of USAA customers stayed with them in 2008. And they have achieved an 82 percent Net Promoter Score, meaning the majority of customers are passionate supporters. What is your version of receiving orders and wearing a flak jacket so you can recreate your customers' lives during employee orientation? Beloved companies have their new hires (no matter what job they're hired for) work in retail or in their warehouses or wherever the customers are at so they can understand customers and get to know their lives. Do you?

Do You
Walk in Your
Customers'
Shoes?

Can you describe a day in the life of your customer?

Do you know what keeps them up at night? You need to understand their life to serve their life.

Do you?

Decide to be REAL.

Amy's Ice Creams Decided
to Make Their Job Application a White Paper Bag.

DECISION INTENT: Find Standouts Among Many Applicants.

Amy's Ice Creams in Austin, Texas, is beloved for two things: the ice cream and the floor show. They are the ice cream equivalent of Seattle's "flying fish." Ice cream scoops are thrown from one worker to another and caught in cups balanced on their chins . . . while standing on one foot . . . hopping. You'll see ice cream slingers sliding across the counters on their knees and bellies. It's a carnival ride in there. Finding people who are fearless and creative enough to come up with stunts like flinging ice cream balls across a room just can't happen in the normal interview process. How exactly do you ask, "Are you a little bit nuts?" You can't. So, at Amy's applicants receive a white paper bag. It must be brought back within a week turned into a creation that tells Amy's about who they are. From this white paper bag, Amy's finds the personalities to fill their shops.

MOTIVATION: Without the Right People, This Is Just Great Ice Cream.

By using a plain white paper bag as its job application, Amy's gets to know the creative soul lurking within the teenaged candidate standing before them. This idea began with an applicant who was given the bag instead of the boilerplate job application because Amy's had run out of the forms. The applicant floated the bag back into the store with helium balloons; inside the bag were items about her life. She got the job. Now for all applicants, this is how Amy's fills their shops with people who make getting an ice cream like going to the circus.

IMPACT: Amy's Exceeds $5 Million in Gross Annual Sales and 1 Million Ice Cream Servings.

The Amy's Ice Creams Web site says, "Amy's looks at 'going out for ice cream' as a total sensory experience that can revitalize a less-than-stellar day." Part of the joy of going to their ice cream shops is wondering what kind of floor show you'll be greeted with. Getting the right people to work at Amy's has spurred their growth from a single location in 1984 to 14 stores 24 years later. In 1984, Amy's served 125,000 servings of ice cream. Today they sell well over 1 million a year, with gross annual sales exceeding $5 million. Like many of the beloved companies, Amy's Ice Creams doesn't advertise. Word of mouth builds the business, and they redirect marketing money to community development, which fuels more word of mouth. Amy's represents the power of the small business owner and how service and exceptional experiences can build their business. Amy's Ice Creams prospers because it revels in being real. In being their kooky, nutty selves. That people love. This translates even to the Amy's Web site, where the front page welcomes you with "Life is uncertain, eat dessert first!" Sound advice.

What's YOUR White Paper Bag?

How do you select the people who will deliver your special blend of magic to customers?

Are your interviews as unique as your company? Do they reflect who you are?

Decide to be REAL.

CD Baby Decided
to Write This E-Mail That's Been Blogged About Since 2003.

DECISION INTENT: Take Care of Customers Like They Take Care of Artists.

CD Baby was born to create an enjoyable and profitable channel to enable independent musicians to sell their music to the public. The company has made it their quest to keep these musicians in business, cutting out the record-producer middleman that prevents many independent musicians from making a living. For example, CD Baby artists receive $6 to $12 per album rather than the $1 to $2 per album received through a distributor or a mainstream record deal. CD Baby carries this commitment to artists through every action, including how they bond and communicate with customers.

MOTIVATION: Straight Talk and Whimsy Make the Business More Fun.

CD Baby has a warm style we see far too rarely in customer communications. And that is to "write like you talk." CD Baby revels in who they are. They must have been having quite a day when they wrote the following e-mail order confirmation. This bit of whimsy goes out confirming all orders. And while it's true some people have seen this message more than once, it's hard not to grin a little, even when reading it a second or third or fourth (CD Baby customers are repeat shoppers) time:

Your CD has been gently taken from our CD Baby shelves with sterilized contamination-free gloves and placed onto a satin pillow. A team of 50 employees inspected your CD and polished it to make sure it was in the best possible condition before mailing. Our packing specialist from Japan lit a candle and a hush fell over the crowd as he put your CD into the finest gold-lined box that money can buy. We all had a wonderful celebration afterwards and the whole party marched down the street to the post office where the entire town of Portland waved "Bon Voyage!" to your package, on its way to you in our private CD Baby jet on this day, Thursday, December 6th. We're all exhausted but can't wait for you to come back to CDBABY.COM!!

IMPACT: CD Baby Paid Over $34 Million to Artists in 2008, Up 28 Percent from 2007.

While whimsical, this note CD Baby sends out to confirm orders gets to the heart of the company's commitment to the 277,000 artists they represent. Thriving since 1998 as one of the largest sellers of independent music on the Web, $4.5 million CDs were sold online to customers. Sales rose 30 percent in 2007. In 2008, while industry CD sales dropped 14 percent overall, CD Baby actually saw an increase of 2 percent. CD Baby bonds with customers by letting down their guard. Do you "write like you talk?"

Is Your Communication "Vanilla"?

Do you have a "voice" that is yours alone?

Would your customers want to know you after reading your letters, your e-mails, your packing slips, or your invoices?

Decide to be REAL.

WestJet Decided
to Make Passengers Human Again.

DECISION INTENT: Make Customers the Reason for the Business.

The dark underbelly of how an industry feels about its customers is often revealed behind the scenes, when colleagues talk to one another. How customers are described and referenced show how much employees and the company honors customers. In the airline business, there's a shorthand language that reduces customers to inanimate objects, not people desiring service. For example, a customer requesting a cup of coffee is reduced to "PAX in 12B wants a coffee." When WestJet began their airline, they decided to nix the lingo and make passengers human again. They wanted "out of the cockpit thinking" to set themselves apart.

MOTIVATION: Earn Market Share in a Noble Manner.

WestJet knew that to win market share, they would have to compete beyond operational efficiency. They would need to compete with their humanity and service. WestJet began by throwing out some bad industry habits. Instead of looking at passengers as walking dollar signs—simply a means to a profit—WestJet decided to treat passengers as valued guests. "Employees" don't exist at WestJet. They are all "WestJetters," a community of people on a common mission. And WestJet executives? Well, they're "Big Shots." Hard to get a big head with a moniker like that. According to Don Bell, executive vice president and cofounder of what is now Canada's number two airline, "I think the simplest way to put it is we applied some very commonsense approaches to piggyback on human nature. We created an environment that embraced people and put people first."

IMPACT: WestJet Is Now Canada's Second Largest Airline.

WestJet decided to grow by offering passengers a new way of flying: By walking away from the old habits that defined working in the airline industry, and then focusing that culture on serving and honoring passengers, WestJet is considered a different kind of airline, one that customers love. Their idea, that the way to grow was through first changing "WestJetters'" mind-sets about their jobs, about themselves, and about customers was rewarded with business growth. In the fourth quarter of 2008, the company posted record revenues. They earned "Canada's Most Admired Corporate Culture" designation by Waterstone Human Capital from 2005 to 2007. How hard would it be for you to remove some of the lingo and attitudes that have built up over years in your industry? Start with your acronyms and see how many of them have to do with customers. That will give you a quick glimpse into the journey ahead.

What
does your
Underbelly
Say about
YOU?

Behind the scenes, how do people talk about customers?

If someone was standing on the other side of the wall with a glass . . . what would they hear?

Decide to be REAL.

Zappos.com Decided to Twitter the Day Away.

DECISION INTENT: Let Customers Know the People of Zappos.com.
Twittering is democratic. No baloney. Good "tweets" are short and sweet. There's no room for any pretense or pomp. Tony (Zappos.com CEO) is a guy who Twitters and he's glad to have you know him as Tony. So do George and Mary and Sue and all the other Zappos.com folks ("Zapponians") sending "tweets" about what's going on in their day. For Zappos.com, Twittering is, plain and simple, about staying in touch with the people in their lives. This naturally includes customers.

MOTIVATION: Zappos.com Wants to Be a Part of Customers' Lives.
Twittering is a natural extension of how Zappos.com exists and participates in people's lives. Zappos people are straight talkers who embrace ten principles to guide how they conduct themselves in business.

1. Deliver WOW through Service
2. Embrace and Drive Change
3. Create Fun and a Little Weirdness
4. Be Adventurous, Creative, Open-Minded
5. Pursue Growth and Learning
6. Build Open and Honest Relationships Through Communication
7. Build a Positive Team, Family Spirit
8. Do More with Less
9. Be Passionate and Determined
10. Be Humble

Twittering is a natural part of the "conversation" Zappos.com has with customers, suppliers, and now, many people around the world. Zappos also responds to "tweets" about them when possible. The folks there feel it's only fitting that they stay in touch and reach out—just as you would if you found a friend who needed to talk to you. Go to http://twitter.com/zappos to join the party and the conversation.

IMPACT: Hundreds of Thousands of People Follow Tony Hsieh on Twitter.
Zappos's growth is fueled by their great products and service. But with Twitter, it goes beyond business to make connections personal. One recent tweet from Tony was "Getting a haircut." Why would anyone want to follow that? Because the commonality of how we go through our days pulls us all together. Following Tony on Twitter creates an unexpected bond. People feel like they know him, so of course they want to buy things from his site. Twitter is deepening Zappos.com's connection beyond their initial fan base of zealot female shoe buyers, helping them to expand (as Amazon.com did) into many other product categories beyond the shoes they originally sold. The company that earned the right with shoes continues to earn the right to expand, in part, by letting people know they're at the dry cleaner.

How do you stay c-o-n-n-e-c-t-e-d?

Companies still jump to surveys and focus groups to find out what their customers need.

All they really need to do is reach out. Do you? Do customers feel like you are people they can talk to? Are you part of their lives in a natural way?

Decide to be REAL.

Trader Joe's Decided
to Manage the "Ping" of Its Cash Register Ring.

DECISION INTENT: Don't Interrupt the Conversations at Checkout.
Trader Joe's wants to be your neighborhood store—a place where you are welcomed by people who want to have a personal relationship with you. That's why Trader Joe's resisted installing scanners as part of its checkout process for years. The hesitation came from concerns over the sound the scanners make, usually a "pinging" noise as each item is scanned. The company didn't want that noise to interrupt the conversations at checkout. Trader Joe's ever-changing and growing inventory mix finally pushed the company to concede to the technology in order to efficiently manage the business. But it wasn't until they were absolutely sure the sound of the "ping" from the scanner didn't interrupt the flow of conversation between cashier and customer.

MOTIVATION: Neighborly Talk Bonds Customers to Trader Joe's.
Trader Joe's wanted to make sure that customers didn't find that the introduction of technology meant the disappearance of personal relationships. Besides being picky about the sound of the checkout system, Trader Joe's also avoids the microphones that are often used by checkout folks to "ask for help in aisle 5." Instead, there are bells at every checkout station. Rung for specific reasons, they represent Trader Joe's version of Morse Code. The Trader Joe's Web site explains: "Those blustery PA systems just didn't feel right to us, so we came up with a simple system to communicate—island style. One bell lets our crew know when to open another register. Two bells mean there are additional questions that need to be answered at the checkout. Three bells call over a manager-type person." The explanation is finished with, "Honestly, it's much easier than the ole message in a bottle trick."

IMPACT: Trader Joe's Fans Won't Move Without Them.
When Trader Joe's fans Ken Vickers and his wife moved to Phoenix, one of the first things they did was find out how close the nearest Trader Joe's was to their home. A blogger on Trader Joe's fan site, who moved from California, says, "Trader Joe's is the one thing I miss most about San Francisco besides the ocean." This almost obsessive attention to detail is critical to Trader Joe's in order for them to deliver on the "TJ" experience. Trader Joe's believes that the sales per square foot that they achieve—which yields revenues triple the square foot sales of a standard supermarket—is testament to the success of their obsession for combining product and customer service to deliver the Trader Joe's experience. Customers flock to the stores. What moments of customer contact are most important for you to obsess about? Do you know?

What gets between you

And your customers?

Do you obsess about the moments of connection? About how you relate? Do you think about not just what you say but how you say it?

Decide to be REAL.

The Container Store Decided
to Be Like Gumby.

DECISION INTENT: Encourage Flexibility and "Gut."

When The Container Store was building their business in 1978, founders Garrett Boone and Kip Tindell wanted to encourage their employees to bend over backward for customers and each other. They wanted to make sure that going the extra mile was core to everybody's actions. So they decided to shorthand this intent by asking everyone to focus on "Being Gumby." A dark green clay figure who came alive through stop motion clay animation, Gumby was the star of *The Gumby Show*, which ran over a 35-year period on American television. Gumby was always getting into some predicament, which he managed to get out of with grace. Not so different from working retail. Makes sense that "Be Gumby" is a favorite mantra at The Container Store.

MOTIVATION: Customers Can Spot a Fake Culture.

Plenty of companies tout their customer service and commitment, but many are "lip service" cultures: all talk, no action. Boone and Tindell wanted to ensure they didn't deliver forced customer "service," defined by rule books and execution of required tasks. The Container Store frees people to trust their judgment and solve customers' problems. But the company also puts them in a position to succeed. A full-time salesperson at The Container Store receives about 241 hours of training, compared to an average of 7 hours for most retail businesses. By preparing people through training and throwing away the rule book, the company wanted to create an environment where people are encouraged to do whatever it takes to assist coworkers and customers. They simply want everyone to be flexible and find the right solution for each situation. Simply put: be flexible, "Be Gumby."

IMPACT: Flexible Employees = Employees Who Stay, in Retail!

At The Container Store, employees feel uninhibited to connect with customers and coworkers in an uncommonly warm and genuine fashion. It's a place where, on a new store's grand-opening day, the chairman pushes the new store manager around on a "victory lap." "Just because we have titles, it doesn't mean we can't still be corny," said Kip Tindell. Corny works for them. This is a company where "I'm being Gumby today" defines success. With only 15 percent voluntary turnover in 2008, compared to an average 50 percent or higher in retail, this is a company where employees want to stay. The Container Store has had a place on *Fortune*'s 100 Best Companies to Work For list for nine years in a row. Does your organization blend whimsy with business and pass on that warmth to customers?

Do you encourage flexibility and "gut"?

Do you give customers a positive view of how the front line is encouraged to do what's right, to work together, and to serve customers?

Decide to be REAL.

CustomInk Decided
to Donate to Every Charity That Buys Their Shirts.

DECISION INTENT: Honor What Customers Care About.

CustomInk is a $60 million T-shirt shop that prints custom T-shirts for family reunions and group and business events. Because actual people at CustomInk personally review every single order, they know what events their products are being printed for. The company saw so many shirts being created for charities that they decided to become personally invested in these causes. So whenever a T-shirt gets printed by CustomInk for a charity event, they send a donation. Done initially as a casual gesture by Lori Mayfield, a CustomInk order analyst, now, Mayfield says, "we try to donate to every charity event that our customers hold close to their hearts."

MOTIVATION: Give Back.
Participate in Customers' Lives.

CustomInk wouldn't feel right printing T-shirts for a charitable organization without giving back to their cause. With this one gesture they let their customers know they back their efforts. What's most important about this gesture is that CustomInk did *not* take this action as a marketing effort. It began as a personal expression by an order analyst who wanted to give back to companies that trusted CustomInk. In the end, like many other noble decisions, it returns to the sender. CustomInk's genuine gesture to contribute to what their customers care about separates them from other T-shirt suppliers. It draws customers back to do business with a company that thinks this way.

IMPACT: Charities Flock to CustomInk. Charity Donations Grew 155 percent from 2008 to 2009.

CustomInk has delivered over 10 million shirts, with 98.9 percent of their customers saying they will purchase from them again. Though their donation to charity customers is small in amount (as little as $30), this gesture connects the company personally with what their customers care about. And it shows customers that their service is not just about getting and filling orders. With this gesture, CustomInk figuratively sticks their hand out of the shipping box and warmly embraces customers. And customers embrace CustomInk in return. Says one: "I definitely was not expecting an e-mail asking if CustomInk could give a donation to our organization. This makes me proud to have picked this company to do our printing for us." And as you can see from the increase in CustomInk's growth in donations, charities are rewarding CustomInk because they care. The percent of CustomInk's charitable donations is directly related to the growth rate they are experiencing in charities flocking to them. How do you connect in that personal manner with your customers?

How do you
show what you're
MADE
OF?

What selfless acts tell your customers and employees about what matters to you?

Decide to be REAL.

Headsets.com Decided
That Disrespect Is a "Fireable" Offense.

DECISION INTENT: Respect Is the Foundation for the Culture of the Company.

The Headsets.com experience is defined by the customer service rep you reach when you call, and how you feel when you hang up the phone. And that experience fuels their growth. At Headsets.com 52 phone reps work with customers, guiding them through the maze of selecting the product that is right for them. At the core of that call is respect. Says founder and CEO Mike Faith, "The customer deserves our respect. Sometimes they could be wrong. But they always deserve our respect." And that's why if any one of those reps rolls his or her eyes, acts exasperated, or does not give customers the respect they deserve, that is the end of that rep's job at Headsets.com.

MOTIVATION: Compromising Culture Hinders Growth.

To ensure that disrespect is a rarity, Headsets.com is very rigorous in how they screen and hire candidates. Before they are hired, candidates go through what Mike Faith calls a day of customer-service tryouts. This includes up to eight interviews. They talk to a voice coach (to check for warmth, tone, and empathy) and a business psychologist, to understand how they react to pressure and how they might, for example, keep their exasperation in check when customer calls get unwieldy. They are tested for memory and English usage and grammar. They sit in on calls. After these initial screens, multiple interviews inside the company determine if they are a "fit" for the Headsets.com culture and customer commitment. This rigor is in place because reps are encouraged to trust their gut in how they interact with customers. And respect is paramount to these interactions. Although rarely acted upon, this commitment of making disrespect a "fireable" offense helps reps who have had a long work shift, or a chatty customer asking obvious questions, remember that customers are entitled to their point of view, to their rant, and to have their say.

IMPACT: $30 Million in Revenue . . . on Headsets!

Headsets.com is, according to Mike Faith, "dedicated to customer love." Respect for customers is at the core of that love. The company is a success because of their ability to sustain service passion. Only 1 in 30 applicants who go through their customer service tryouts make it into the company as a Headsets.com rep. And once you're there, customer respect rules. Rigorous? Absolutely. But effective? Something must be working. This company focusing on selling headsets grew from a $40,000 investment in 1998 to $30 million in revenue in 2008.

Is MUTUAL RESPECT a core competency?

Are you great at finding and nurturing people who develop and earn customer respect? How rigorously do you screen the folks who will become your company to your customers?

Decide to be REAL.

What's Your Story: How "Real" Are You?

The beloved companies aren't afraid to be themselves. They give employees permission to drop the "corporate veneer" and encourage them to take the best version of themselves to work and into their relationships with customers.

They work hard to eliminate the feeling of "big company" and "little customer." From The Container Store, who urges their people to act so flexible that they give a "Gumby" award, to WestJet's self-effacing title of "Big Shot" for their executives, the people inside these companies take their work seriously but not themselves. They revel in letting their warmth come through.

Setting the tone and giving "permission" to be this real are often the leaders inside these companies, who make it okay for everyone to do the same. At LUSH, founder Mark Constantine sets the tone for the conversations with customers. At Headsets.com, founder Mike Faith is the zealot. Even after their founders leave, beloved companies work to keep the vibe going. Trader Joe's has stayed entrenched in their culture, even after founder Joe Coulombe retired in 1988, and then even when it was sold to German entrepreneur Theo Albrecht. In the hand-off between three CEOs—from Coulombe to John Shields and now to Dan Bane—Trader Joe's has stayed true to who they are, to what connected them to their legions of fan-customers.

The language and communication a customer receives from the beloved companies is straightforward and uncluttered. This communication is often so unexpected that the messages they send take on a viral life of their own, such as the order confirmation sent to customers by CD Baby. Humility, at times humor, and, almost always, lack of pretense or protocol define personal interactions with people inside the beloved companies, because they've been encouraged to be themselves. You only have to be on one or two Southwest Airlines flights to know how much the company celebrates the humorist in their employees and encourages them to bring that to work with them. By being willing to work "without a net" of corporate language and protocol, the beloved companies opt to build relationships between people.

They work hard to connect with what we all have in common. As people.

These decisions and actions embody what is behind the beloved companies who are authentic and real. They take what informs their personal decisions with them into business. They let their roots influence decision making. People call

"Beloved companies work hard to eliminate the feeling of 'big company' and 'little customer.'"

upon their personal experiences to inform their behavior. And they blend it with their business acumen to accomplish extraordinary outcomes.

Companies who decide to be real pull customers and employees to them. Where are you today?

- Do leaders blend who they are as people with how they lead?
- Would you want to read your invoices, bills, or contracts?
- How are customers greeted when they call your company?
- Are people scripted or guided?
- Do you discuss customers or contracts? Insurance policies or families?

Do You...

Touch a chord with customers?

Encourage personality and creativity of employees?

Communicate personally, without the corporate veneer?

Make decisions by envisioning customers in their lives?

How would customers describe who you are as people?

How do employees describe your company personality?

What's Your Story:
How "Real" Are You?

For a tool kit on how to use these questions to improve your business, go to www.customerbliss.com.

5

Decide

to **BE THERE**

The middle of the road is where the white line is
and that's the worst place to drive.

—Robert Frost

It's an everyday charge up the hill to be there for customers in ways that are important to them. Beloved companies gladly decide to do the hard work. They're in the scrimmage every day to earn the right for their customers to return.

Being there for customers fuels the prosperity engine of beloved companies. Beloved companies think and rethink how to conduct themselves, so they earn the right to their customers' continued business. Their "experience" is far more than the execution of an operating plan. They leave customers thinking, "Who else would have done this?" "Where else could I get this?" "I want to do this again." By creating reliability in the way they do business, and fusing that with moments of contact delivered from the customer's point of view, beloved companies earn the right to grow

Beloved Companies Decide to Be There.

"We must earn the right to continued relationships with customers."

Amazon.com sold its first book in July 1995. The success of that experience earned the company the right to add a music store in 1998, and consumer electronics and toys and games in 1999. Since then, the addition of nearly every category has been met with customer acceptance: a kitchen store, a camera and photo store, office products, apparel, sporting goods, gourmet foods, even health and personal care and high-end jewelry. If Amazon.com had not executed the delivery of books well during its foundational years, its expansion into these other lines could not have occurred. Amazon.com continues to operate with the understanding that customer loyalty is a right that must be earned—it is not an entitlement. Named the most reliable e-tailer for the 2008 holiday shopping season, Amazon.com's results attest to the power of being there for customers. Giving customers peace of mind for what to expect fueled their business growth.

Companies that earn customers' trust and peace of mind often create the emotion of *desire* for their experience. Customers look forward to repeating their experience. While buying books over the Internet is old hat to us now, when Amazon.com was first introduced to us, our lives changed. They delivered the joy of receiving books in the comfort of our living rooms. And not just with their operational finesse, but also with the thoughtfulness with which they delivered what was in our shopping carts. We wanted to repeat the experience again and again.

Beloved Companies Deliver What Customers *Desire*.

The *Journal of Consumer Research* says in its article "The Fire of Desire: A Multisited Inquiry in Consumer Passion" that "there is spreading consensus that much, if not all, consumption has been quite wrongly characterized as involving need fulfillment, utility maximization, and reasoned choices." Think of services or experiences you've had that were astounding in how they impacted you. There is a desire to repeat those experiences—most likely not only because of the utility of what was delivered, but because of how you were related to, and treated, and made to feel.

Let's say, for example, that a company is in the business of making plastic drinking cups for children. While on the surface this may sound like a trivial matter, it is not, as anyone with children knows. The right drinking cup can play a leading role in getting a child to sleep and making mealtime a relatively peaceful endeavor. Traditional customer focus groups determine what type of cup a company should manufacture by bringing a group of customers together and placing several on the table. The facilitators ask every customer, "Which cup do you prefer?" Each customer then picks a cup. But that doesn't mean any cup is best for them. Maybe one customer needs a cup with a straw, but the company didn't take the time to learn about their customers' lives. In the absence of getting what was right, customers picked what was available.

Beloved companies start with the customer instead of the cup. They yearn to understand the emotions of the young mom who is buying the cup—to understand what solution she'd *desire* rather than just settle for. They learn about her life and what she needs and then build a solution from her point of view. Product development solutions made on autopilot are turned on their ear when customer needs, emotions, and desires become the inspiration for product and service development. Within the beloved companies, their curiosity for understanding customer emotions in every interaction informs decision making.

> "The everyday company is selling cups.
>
> "The beloved company is supporting parenthood."

As consumers, we're conditioned to take what's available. Beloved companies work hard every day to put a stop to that. They go beyond executing tasks. They're in it to deliver an experience their customers *desire*. Even how they learn what customers yearn for sets them apart. In this instance, it is not the utility of buying a cup that compels a young mother to go shopping; it's her desire to help her child's development, or to get him or her to sleep, or to not have to wipe up the floor 20 times a day. The companies that go beyond meeting the obvious utility of "needing a cup," as in this example, reach the underlying emotions and needs of their customers. These companies build lasting bonds with their customers. They are the ones remembered with fondness long after the children are grown, because for a period of time they were an important part of their customers' lives.

A simple way to remember this is: the everyday company is selling cups; the beloved company is supporting parenthood. Beloved companies learn customers' aspirations, needs, and desires and become a part of their lives. By being there for customers, on their terms, they earn the right to have their story told by legions of customers who want others to experience what they've experienced. They earn the right to grow.

Companies that have this mind-set immediately grow. They grow organically from word of mouth. Their stories are told over and over again by legions of customers who urge others to try them. And this is not limited to only consumer business. Since it was founded, business-to-business company Rackspace, which manages the technology backbone of clients as diverse as e-commerce retailers, game sites, and online ad agencies, has experienced 50 percent growth year after year. Most impressive is that their growth is organic. Rackspace grows primarily through word of mouth from loyal customers who are fanatical about the service they receive.

Rackspace grows by imagining the life of IT managers who have to decide whether they should host and build their own Web sites or entrust the job to someone else. Rackspace understands that people who choose Web hosting want someone else to be responsible for their servers, period. They not only want to outsource the servers, they want to outsource the responsibility that comes with them when something goes wrong (which it inevitably does). Rackspace was the first hosting company (and there are lots of them) to understand that and to wire that into the company's DNA. Clients stake their reputations every day on reliable Web site and back-office operations. By being there on the customers' terms, Rackspace has changed the face of IT hosting support, and has earned the right to customers telling its story.

One popular story told involves Rackspace Tech Support Manager Simon Newman. While on a date with his fiancée, Newman received a call from a frantic customer. Someone had hacked into the servers powering his client's Web sites. His entire business and reputation were at stake. Simon interrupted his date and met the customer at his office, calmly "peeled him off the wall," and got to work. In 4 hours he accomplished a feat that usually takes 24—building a new server. Committed to getting the job done, he jumped in his car and delivered the newly constructed server across town to the data center himself rather than turning the job over to a courier. Throughout the night, Simon enlisted Rackspace technicians to get the new server and his customer's business operational again.

Rackspace calls this "fanatical support." And it's required behavior to stay on the job and grow. Rackspace puts itself in the shoes of its customers and then architects an experience from their point of view. The technology marketplace is full of service providers and tech support staff. But most don't deliver the reliability and passion that Rackspace customers receive. Fanatical support fuels Rackspace's growth.

> **"Each beloved company makes key decisions to mark its place in the universe with customers."**

For another company, performing a mundane task in customers' lives is its growth engine. 1-800-GOT-JUNK? has become the largest junk removal company in the world based on the fundamental idea of "being there." By considering how people usually experience this household chore and offering them the alternative of a reliable service experience, they have become the largest junk hauling company in the world.

1-800-GOT-JUNK? founder Brian Scudamore imagined customers' lives as they tried to get rid of their junk. So he decided to become the "The FedEx of Junk." For him that meant emulating the reliability of FedEx. When you call 1-800-GOT-JUNK? you know what to expect, when you'll get the service, how the people will appear and act. Customers book online (www.1800gotjunk.com) or by calling their toll-free number. When you call the "Junktion," there is a pleasant operator standing by to take your call. Customers can designate a two-hour period for pickup. What pulls up to your house at the scheduled time of your junk removal appointment is not a rusty, dusty truck with a dragging muffler, but a shiny blue Isuzu truck buttoned up to hide the sight of the junk. And what steps out from the truck is a set of uniformed, gloved workers who have attended the equivalent of the charm school of junk! When they're done loading your junk, they sweep your garage, basement, or attic—wherever the debris was removed from. They separate out recyclable materials and will take care of disposing challenging items like car batteries. It's an unexpectedly good experience. Even memorable.

Are You There for Your Customers? On Their Terms?

What follows is the deconstruction of a set of decisions made by companies across multiple industries. Beloved companies make decisions with an understanding that they must constantly earn the right to their continued relationships. And that starts with being there when customers need them, on their terms.

In each of these cases, companies were able to reach uncommon decisions that connected them with customers because they:

- Imagined their customers' lives.
- Were clear on their purpose for delivering a solution to their lives.
- Built their experience from the customers' point of view.
- Executed with operational reliability.

For beloved companies, how customers live their lives informs and inspires their behavior, their actions, and the operation of the business. The interactions customers have with a company tell them how much forethought was put into how they cross the paths of their lives. Reliability fuels customer stories about their experiences with the companies they love. Having the ability to make decisions in this manner is within your reach.

The Decision Is Yours.

Zara Decided
to Invest in Product Speed, Not Advertising.

DECISION INTENT: Create "Fast Fashion."

Zara wants to get a product from inception to market—inside a store on a rack and available to their zealot customers—within 15 days. This speedy process for bringing in product and changing out inventory creates an on-purpose product extinction cycle, and a compelling draw for customers to constantly visit Zara stores. "Fast Fashion" is Zara's customer magnet. It brings customers into stores to see what is new, what they must not miss, and what they must own before it's gone forever. Speed of fashion for Zara also means having an agility for listening to and responding to customer requests in the marketplace. Inditex, Zara's parent company, says that an item requested by enough customers can be in their stores to accommodate that request within ten days.

MOTIVATION: Pull Customers Back into the Stores with "Fast Fashion."

Zara's understanding of customers drives its decisions for how it designs, produces product, and stocks its stores. Zara works to appeal to the emotional desire of "fashionistas" to be one of the first and one of the few to own a particular item of clothing. This emotional desire pulls customers back into the stores; it is their magnet for customer repurchasing. To constantly earn this devotion, Zara's "Fast Fashion" operation integrates design, manufacturing, and distribution, all managed from their headquarters outside La Coruña, Spain. To create exclusivity, they produce small batches of each style. Three hundred designers work to create the continuous stream of new looks in their stores, resulting in 20,000 new designs a year.

Zara wants customers coming back into their stores, where they will always find new products, in limited quantities. This is how Zara creates urgency to buy *now*. The blue blouse she loves today may be gone tomorrow.

IMPACT: Customers Visit Zara 17 Times a Year!

By understanding what motivates its "fashionista" customers, Zara has changed the definition of success in fashion retail. Customers make an average 17 annual store visits, compared to 4 visits for other retailers. The Zara "habit" that keeps customers coming through their door results in more products sold at full retail: nearly 85 percent of Zara's inventory sells at full price, compared to a retail average of 40 percent. Most important, because customers are Zara's sales force, advertising is hardly necessary—it's a mere .3 percent of sales, compared to competitors' 3 to 4 percent. How much do you know about your customers' lives and what makes them tick? What's your version of "fast fashion" for your customers?

Do you know

your customers?

Does how they go through their day inspire and inform the actions you take?

Do you plan for how you impact their lives based on how they live them?

Decide to BE THERE.

Umpqua Bank Decided
to Enable Customizable Banking.

DECISION INTENT: Support People's Lives, Not Execute Banking Tasks.

Umpqua Bank is committed to delivering an experience customized for each customer. Steve May, Umpqua's executive vice president of "cultural enhancement," has a goal that everybody in every store is able to do every task. Umpqua wants a teller who can take a mortgage application and a loan officer who is pleased to help with a safety deposit box. Beyond the banking experience, Umpqua believes in customizing experiences by community. The company leaves it to the managers in each community bank to customize their offerings based on their customers and their interests—from yoga classes in one "store" location (they don't use the word "branch") to movie nights or a knitting club in another. Each has its own fund to enable it to customize the experience based on the lives of the customers in its community.

MOTIVATION: Make Umpqua a Community Destination.

Umpqua's mission is to become a destination for customers. By offering a warm environment customized by community interests and a banking experience personalized to every customer who walks through their doors, it wants customers to think of the Umpqua bank in their community as *their* store, their gathering place. An unexpected place where they can go to listen to music and have a cup of coffee, or take a yoga class! Umpqua stores should feel more like a neighborhood gathering place than a bank.

IMPACT: Staff Turnover Is Half the Banking Industry Average.

As Umpqua changed its approach from a traditional "banking"-style service to a customized experience for each customer, employees had to learn to juggle many duties. It meant more work initially, but now they can't imagine being limited to the individual tasks their jobs were defined as previously. As Umpqua has grown from 6 to 148 stores, with staff increases from 350 to 1,800, it has retained its focus on the customer and the values that built the bank. And the company has retained its employees. Umpqua's voluntary employee turnover rate is just 20 percent, compared to the banking industry rate of about 40 percent. In 2008, as a testament that this change in focus was not only good for customers but also great for employees, the company made, for the second year in a row, *Fortune* magazine's list of the "100 Best Companies to Work For." How good are the jugglers in your business? Does your environment embrace and welcome customers? How can you make a visit to your business a welcome oasis during your customer's day?

Do customers look forward *to seeing you?*

Are your operating decisions based on executing tasks or **delivering an experience** *that complements your customer's day?*

Decide to BE THERE.

Zane's Cycles Decided
to Give Away Parts Costing Less Than $1.

DECISION INTENT: Become Their Customers' "Go to" Place.

Picture a dad on a Saturday morning toting a bike with a broken chain and a disappointed kid. Dad's already been to the hardware store, with no luck. Two stops later, exasperated and increasingly frustrated, both father and son find their way to Zane's. Within minutes they find out what will fix the chain: a twenty-five-cent master link. The salesman at Zane's hands it over, with a firm "No charge." Zane's has decided to give these parts away. Anything that costs a buck or under, they give to any customer who needs it. Though small in price, these parts are usually attached to a frustrating experience for the customer. Says Chris Zane: "I could either charge the guy one buck or two bucks for the part or give it to him. So I give the part away, along with an extra one."

MOTIVATION: Make Seven Good Impressions—It Keeps Customers Connected.

Zane's wants to become the lifeline for their customer throughout his or her bike ownership. And that sometimes means throwing in a bike part—especially at frustrating moments. Zane's wants to build strong relationships through creating indelible memories, like the one that made the day of that father and son. Chris Zane is astute enough to know that in these moments, an emotional bond to his store is created. And this will translate in the future into a prosperous customer relationship. Zane's works to deliver at least seven "wow" moments for each customer. They do this because at Zane's they believe that seven powerful interactions prove to customers that Zane's is (a) consistently good to them, and (b) the best (and only) place to go for anything regarding bicycles. Why does Zane's do this? Because it's the right thing to do. And because they have a track record of success with these acts of kindness. Zane's "pays it forward" consistently with their customers, and it grows their business.

IMPACT: By Extending Human Kindness, Zane's Wins Market Share.

The memories customers have of that point in time when they were stressed and Zane's came through, with no strings attached, pulls them back to them. And once a customer walks back into Zane's, he or she usually buys. Each Zane's customer spends an average of $12,500 with the company. So you do the math: wouldn't you spend $1 to make an impression that will earn a customer worth $12,500? How many "wow" impressions do you encourage your people to deliver in the course of a day, a month, or a year to your customers? Consider if those nickel, dime, and dollar charges are costing you more than you're charging in lost goodwill and future customers.

Have you planned for heroic acts of kindness?

Is everyone ready to go the extra mile?

Do they have permission?

Do you celebrate their heroism every day?

Decide to BE THERE.

Newegg.com Decided
to Display Only Products It Can Ship Immediately.

DECISION INTENT: It Won't Make Promises It Can't Keep.

Newegg.com is loved, from technical wizards to those who are just beginning to introduce technology into their lives. A big reason for this adoration is because it tells the truth about its inventory to customers. The minute its warehouse runs out of an item, Newegg.com marks that product as unavailable on the Web page or it is removed from their site. Newegg .com breaks from the frequent practice of electronics and technology retailers who offer an extensive inventory, feigning depth and availability of product. Often those other retailers order the item from the supplier only *after* the customer places an order. As anyone who's experienced this practice knows, the benefit is all on the side of the merchant, not the customer. They've got the customer's money, and those other merchants have checked "fulfillment" of the order off their list. But the customer is left waiting, and waiting, and waiting.

MOTIVATION: Grow Through Delivery Reliability for Customers.

Newegg.com knows their customers start watching the clock as soon as they place the order with them. So Newegg .com commits to delivery reliability. If you can place an order for an item on their site, you are guaranteed that it is on its way to you. This contrasts greatly with many online computer and electronics retailers who continue to take orders just to collect revenue and then put customers into a back-order waiting game! Taking a customer's money without knowing when they can deliver is something Newegg.com just won't do.

IMPACT: Newegg.com Has Grown to 11 Million Registered Customers Since 2001.

Since their first order was placed in 2001, Newegg.com has grown to 11 million registered customers. And it's not just because of their inventory; the Newegg experience is about reliability, commitment, and community. An average of 600,000 daily visitors go to the Web site to chat with the swarming masses of folks on their boards, but they also go there to place orders. Newegg.com ships over 40,000 orders a day. Their customers can count on Newegg.com, so they stick with the company. Most important, customers show their love with sales. The second largest online-only retailer in the United States, in 2007 Newegg.com sold approximately $1.9 billion of products. On the day after Thanksgiving 2008, a day traditionally seen as an indicator of the strength of the important holiday season, more than triple the number of buyers from 2007 purchased from Newegg.com. In December 2008, the company recorded a year-over-year growth of 178 percent compared to an industry average of only 1 percent.

Do you
accept the order
and
the
responsibility?

*Customers trust that you
can meet their needs when
they need them met.*

*Are you as quick to fulfill
orders as your customers
expect and deserve?*

Decide to BE THERE.

Commerce Bank (Now TD Bank) Decided to Put Penny Arcades in Its Stores.

DECISION INTENT: Create a Bit of Theater in the Stores.

Ever try taking that jar of accumulating nickels, dimes, quarters, and pennies to a bank to have it turned into rolls or exchanged it for paper currency? Most banks require that you have an account before they take your money. And even if you have an account, there are numerous rules for how to wrap it, roll it, and label it. Fees, of course, apply to every roll. Commerce Bank (now TD Bank) wanted to get rid of all of that and simply help anybody out who had a bunch of change to get rid of—whether you banked with them or not.

MOTIVATION: The Penny Arcade Is a Service Magnet That Creates Customers.

TD Bank thinks of its penny arcade as a service magnet. It brings people in, and introduces them to the bank. The bank knew that besides making change, they would be making friends. So a penny arcade exists in every store, and it's part of the entertainment of being there. There is no fee to use it, and there is no requirement to be a customer. But there is immediate gratification when the machine gulps down your change and spits out a receipt. Of course, the receipt is immediately redeemable for cash, which you can put in your account or use to open up a new account.

IMPACT: Five Million People Went into Commerce Bank in 2007 for the Penny Arcade.

In 2007, this service magnet attracted five million customers and noncustomers into the bank to watch the show, experience the service, and possibly become a customer. It's impossible to translate the impact of this one gesture on branch openings and growth. But this fact is compelling: within ten minutes of walking into this bank for the first time to use the free arcade, a penny arcade user can have a new account set up and ready to use. They perfected this process and speed out of necessity from the amount of requests received from Penny Arcade users to open an account. From the lines out the door to use the arcade some days, it's clear that the Penny Arcade is a service magnet. In three years, from 2004 to 2007, Commerce Bank (now TD Bank) nearly doubled its number of branches, from 96 to 185

What's Your Service Magnet?

What can you do to let customers know of your sincerity to serve them?

What gesture can you offer that helps your customers and draws them to you?

Decide to BE THERE.

Threadless.com Decided to Give Customers Control.

DECISION INTENT: Let Customers Submit the Designs They Want to Wear.

Threadless.com began in 2000 after artist Jake Nickell won a T-shirt design contest in an online forum called "Dreamless." Dreamless was a site Nickell often frequented, where he shared his designs with fellow illustrators and programmers, who would post designs back and forth, critiquing each other's work and informally competing for the best designs produced. Nickell wondered, "What if the best designs in the Dreamless community could be printed on T-shirts and sold?"

MOTIVATION: Customer Ownership in Product Design Ensures Success.

In the beginning, the "Threadless" community was created to give artists and designers a place to submit their design ideas and give those designs a home—on the unexpected canvas of a T-shirt. This idea exploded into a fast-growing community reaching far outside the initial graphic and computer-designer circles that first came to Threadless.com. Customers embraced the idea of being involved in the design, the selection, and the purchasing of the products they had a hand in creating. As a result, the Threadless.com community exploded far beyond a small cluster of Web designers to hundreds of thousands of zealot customers. The idea of having designers submit ideas for T-shirt designs, and then giving customers a vote in what gets sold, struck a nerve. A big, profitable nerve. In their first two years, the Threadless.com community swelled to over 100,000. Since then, it has grown to over 700,000 members.

IMPACT: Every Single Product Eventually Sells Out.

Threadless.com has become a company of the customer, by the customer, for the customer. It has grown tenfold from 70,000 members at the end of 2004 to over 700,000 members in 2008. Customers are in the driver's seat, submitting the designs, voting on the shirts, buying them, talking to one another, and even working at the company. And because customers vote on the designs, and therefore decide which T-shirts are sold, every single product eventually sells out. Threadless.com sold more than $30 million in T-shirts in 2008—with a 30 percent profit margin. Revenue growth is approximately 200 percent per year, with no help from professional designers, advertising, modeling agencies, or a sales force. How do you engage your customers? Do you seek their validation after the decisions have been made, or are customers truly part of how you imagine, build, and deliver your products and services?

Can you **blur** the line between customer and company?

Beloved companies tap the passionate energy of their customers to grow and prosper by encouraging participation in building products and services they need and desire.

Do customers have a seat at your table and a hand in design?

Decide to BE THERE.

Edward Jones Decided
Senior Advisors Should Give Away Their Accounts.

DECISION INTENT: Ensure New Advisors Are Mentored for Success.

At Edward Jones, experienced financial advisors give away a portion of their accounts to help their newest colleagues get started. Freshly minted advisors are paired with a successful veteran for at least a year, allowing them to share in the operation of the branch, receive invaluable mentoring from the veteran they are paired with, and assume responsibility for some of the veteran's accounts. This assures that before a new advisor opens his or her own branch, that advisor has modeled the best behavior, and has built relationships with clients he or she will take over from the veteran.

MOTIVATION: Continuity of Service Builds and Grows Customer Relationships.

In this one single decision, Edward Jones's core values of cooperation, caring, and volunteerism converge. Created by successful financial advisor Jim Goodknight in 1996, this process helps young colleagues successfully launch their careers. Nearly half of all new financial advisors start through what is now referred to as the Goodknight Program, or through similar coaching processes. Veteran financial advisors find it not only good for incoming advisors, but also for clients, who receive "double coverage" by both the veteran and the new advisors during the mentorship period. Veterans are also motivated to see the firm grow, gain market share, and thrive, particularly because Edward Jones is a partnership business. They have a vested interest in doing what's best for growth, even if it means channeling clients from the veteran's book of business to incoming advisors.

IMPACT: Internal Collaboration Is Rewarded by Customers.

Clients involved in a Goodknight Program are more likely to be advocates for Edward Jones. The firm retains more new advisors, who achieve greater success. Veterans focus more on fewer clients, deepening those relationships. Customers take notice of this behavior and reward it. As a result, Edward Jones experiences only a 9 percent voluntary employee turnover rate. Edward Jones ranks 50 points higher than average full-service brokers overall in *BusinessWeek*'s Customer Service Elite, ranking in sixth and eighth place respectively in 2007 and 2008. The Goodknight decision is one of many that have placed the company on the *Fortune* "100 Best Companies to Work For" list every year since 2006; it ranked second on the list in 2009. Corporate collaboration is a quality of the companies customers love. Would your veteran account reps be predisposed to this behavior? What would you have to do to get from where you are today to this state of collaboration?

When Your Service Providers Change…

Do You Provide Continuity of Service?

Beloved companies lock customers in their corporate memory. They honor them by ensuring continuity for serving their needs.

Do you make customers begin again? *Does service continue when accountability changes hands?*

Decide to BE THERE.

Rackspace Decided
to Eliminate Silos for Customers.

DECISION INTENT: Eliminate "Customer Hot Potato" Service.

San Antonio–based Rackspace grows by imagining the life of their IT manager clients. And that means making it easy to get help, support, and service without the customer "hot potato." So Rackspace is organized by teams assigned by customer account, in order to create customer peace of mind. Rackspace's Web site explains this commitment: "No more call centers. No more dealing with a different person every time you need something. No more transferring you to the 'expert' who transfers you to another 'expert.' . . . And, most important, no more feeling like you're just one more anonymous customer stuck in a system that works against you instead of for you."

MOTIVATION: Unify Accountability for Customer Growth.

With this decision, Rackspace is there for clients, on their terms, with a reliable delivery method they can count on. Teams are assembled to include everyone a client needs: account managers, engineers, support technicians, billing, and data center professionals. Everyone on the team has a common set of goals aligned to the client's goals. And they are all rewarded and recognized together—with shared accountability—for ensuring the customer's needs are met. This team structure ensures that when the client

calls their account manager, ready resources are available to support the client. The traditional silos that create the "hot potato" experience are gone. So the client doesn't have to figure out who to call for what and when. Rackspace connects the team to give customers peace of mind.

IMPACT: In 11 Years, Rackspace Grew from a $34 Million to a $1.4 Billion Company.

Serving a diverse customer base of 53,500 worldwide, Rackspace's growth is fueled by "being there" for IT managers. They understand that people who choose IT hosting want someone else to be responsible for their servers, period. By reliably and seamlessly managing the hosting of Web sites so that their clients can stay focused on their businesses, Rackspace has earned the right to grow. It concluded 2008 with significant growth in both revenues and net income, and has experienced revenue growth of 59 percent annually over the last five years. Revenues grew from $139 million at the end of 2005 to $531.9 million at the end of 2008. They have turned a profit during this entire period. Do you make customers traverse your organization chart to do business with you? Would your customers say that they are handed off to many people before they eventually receive help?

Can Everyone
Jump ᵃ Fence
To Serve A Customer?

*Do the boundary lines of your
organization chart keep people
from going the extra mile?*

*Do people care more about where
they sit or how they matter?*

Decide to BE THERE.

Zipcar Decided
to Go to School with College Students.

DECISION INTENT: Get College Students Mobile.

Zipcar was founded in 1999 to break the mold on car rentals by making cars accessible by the hour—and by making that experience quirky and cool. With one foot in "cool" and one foot in "ecofriendly," Zipcar has become a game changer. Gaining ground most rapidly with the under-35-year-old driver, Zipcar blends technology, community, and personality. Yale student Lisa calls it "a new cult of transportation." The need for wheels without the resources for owning a car has been a perennial dilemma of college students and young professionals. Zipcar wanted to provide the solution. And they wanted to do it in a way that appealed to waves of collegians and professionals reared on technology, increasing gas prices, and the power of community. The solution itself is game changing—zip in and out of a parking spot near your dorm without going anywhere but the Internet to do the paperwork.

MOTIVATION: College Students Are Early Adopters. Their Memories Pull Others In.

Scott Griffith, Zipcar's CEO, says, "We're borrowing from Apple's early days when it went after students to be its early adopters." Their goal is to change the traditional rite of passage of buying a car when you graduate. Zipcar yearns to develop a relationship early, by offering cars to college kids who want to drive. So

available rental cars include Mini Coopers for fun and BMW 5-Series for looking like the success they aspire to be after college. Zipcar's goal is to connect with customers early in their car-driving experience and hold them close through adulthood. Playing to the college student's desire for instant gratification, the Zipcar experience is a perfect fit. CEO Griffith has said about the experience, "Getting a car is as easy as getting cash from an ATM."

IMPACT: "Zipster" Fan Base Has Grown to 250,000 Members.

Since 1999, "Zipster" members have grown to 250,000 passionate users and ambassadors. College students have taken to Zipcar, which has a presence now at 100 college and university campuses throughout North America and London, and an inventory of 5,500 self-service vehicles. More than a dozen metropolitan areas have taken to the idea. In an experimental partnership with Starbucks, Zipcar urged people to live a "Low Car Diet," and to try them out. Fifty-eight percent of people who participated said they were hooked and would not go back to vehicle ownership. According to Zipcar COO Mark Norman, it is averaging 10,000 new customers a month. If your customers look back on the part of their lifetime when they used your products, will you be remembered?

Is your experience memorable?

Do you know the moments in your customers' lives when they need you most? Do you dedicate any part of your experience to those moments?

Will you be there?

Decide to BE THERE.

What Story Do Your Decisions Reveal?
Are You There for Customers?

Do you want to be loved by customers? Imagine them in their lives. Get to know them. Understand what is important to them. And obsess about the moments when you intersect their life. Then deliver something that makes those moments better. With your actions, show customers that you make decisions with their point of view in mind. When you do, they'll buy more from you. And tell everyone they know.

Beloved companies won't operate from the middle of the road of indecision and noncommitment. They spend their days (and nights) obsessing about how to be there for customers on the customers' terms. They imagine customers' lives. And they think and rethink how they will conduct themselves so they can constantly earn the right to customers' continued business.

Companies that understand that it is emotions that bond them with customers obsess about getting to know who their customers are and what they desire. When they tap into these emotions and desires, they open up a world of possibilities that can capture the imagination of their business. And that leads to uncommon decisions that separate them from the pack. It grows their business.

Remember, the everyday company is selling cups. The beloved company is supporting parenthood. They share in customers' aspirations and dreams. And become a part of their lives. Are you there for your customers? Do you earn the right to their future business?

Where are you today on deciding to be there for your customers?

- Do you begin with the customer or the product?
- Are your meetings spent discussing sales goals or customers' lives?
- Do you imagine a day in the life of your customers?
- Do you understand their lives so you can improve their lives?
- Are you selling cups or supporting parenthood?

Are You There for Customers...

Do your customers' lives inform and inspire the behavior, the actions, and the operation of your business?

Is your operating plan based on your priorities or customer priorities?

Can customers easily tell the story of the experience you deliver?

What's Your Story:
Are You THERE for Your Customers?

For a tool kit on how to use these questions to improve your business, go to www.customerbliss.com.

6

Decide
to **SAY SORRY**

In the course of my life, I have often had to eat my
words, and I must confess that I have always found
it a wholesome diet.

—Winston Churchill

How you apologize is your humanity litmus test. It is unavoidable that at some point, your business will suffer a failure that disappoints customers. How your company reacts, explains, removes the pain, and takes accountability for actions signals how you think about customers, and the collective heart of your organization. Grace and wisdom guide decisions of beloved companies toward accepting responsibility and resolving the situation when the chips are down—not accusations and skirting accountability. Repairing the emotional connection well is a hallmark of companies that we love. It makes us love them even more.

When a beloved company apologizes for something that goes wrong, the intent and motivation is to make customers whole—to earn the right to continue the relationship. However, repairing the emotional connection with customers in distress can be costly. Often the easy-to-execute apology is extended, but the intent is to only "get past the incident." Beloved companies don't consider the job done until the emotional connection with customers is restored. They turn "recovery" into an opportunity that says to customers, "Who else would respond this way?"

> **"Repairing the emotional connection [with customers] well is a hallmark of companies that we love. It makes us love them even more."**

Many companies consider the apology as admitting defeat. A zero-sum game where someone wins and someone loses, as noted by Aaron Lazare in *On Apology*. When the customer wins their apology, the company loses. In actuality, the reverse is true. A well-executed apology, one that is timely and delivered with humility and remorse, with an olive branch to repair the severed connection, often builds a much stronger relationship. *Both* customer and company win.

In a world globalized through technology, not only the content and tone of a company's apology is crucial, but also the speed at which they apologize. For example, when Apple lowered the price of its new iPhone after only a few weeks on the market, within *minutes* the blogosphere was filled with chatter about the decision. Early iPhone fans who had stood in long lines to be the first to receive it were startled that the price was lowered so quickly after its release. In response to the hundreds of e-mails he received, Apple CEO Steve Jobs extended an apology and a $100 store credit toward the purchase of any product at an Apple store or the Apple Online Store. But that misstep in not communicating the new pricing to early iPhone customers was heard around the world. Make a move inside your company, and very rapidly customers and others impacted will have heard about it, and will be talking about it.

Beloved Companies Decide to Say Sorry.

"We act with humility when things go wrong. We will make it right."

Robert Wright, in his book, *Nonzero: The Logic of Human Destiny,* explains that we would all be better served by looking at solutions from a "nonzero" perspective, meaning there doesn't have to be a "winner" and a "loser." Wright's assertion is that because of our interdependence with others, whether they are companies and their customers or family members, non-zero-sum game solutions are the most ideal. This holds true in business. Companies that are beloved don't take apologizing as admitting defeat. It's part of the journey toward becoming a better company.

Apologizing well for operational gaffes, service blunders, and widespread tragedies or missteps drives company prosperity because, when done well, these apologies strengthen the bond between customer and company. They define the people inside the company, their values and who they are. In a thoughtful and well-executed apology, the focus is on restoring and preserving the relationship; it is about the people impacted and the human connection with them.

The manner in which these companies decide to acknowledge and repair the mistake is done in a non-zero-sum manner. Both sides win. Customers feel they have been honored, acknowledged, and taken care of. Companies continue to prosper. These solutions appeal to the natural order of humanity. They become a peace process where both sides win. Apologizing well is an important "peace process" between companies and their customers.

> **"Apologizing well is an important 'peace process' between companies and their customers."**

The apology peace process between companies and customers is comprised of five actions that signal to customers that they are important and that someone is looking after them:

- Delivering a swift response.
- Showing humility and empathy for what the customer is experiencing.
- Accepting accountability.
- Providing an honest explanation of what happened and a commitment to improve.
- Extending an olive branch—to right the situation and mend the relationship.

The beloved companies are not only good at the apology, but, importantly, are also adept at making the other four decisions outlined in this book. All contribute to their delivery of a meaningful apology. That is why deciding to "say sorry" is the final decision of this book. In challenging times, beloved companies make decisions grounded in humility and grace, offering resolutions that honor customers, and show an intention to mend the relationship.

Belief enables a company to make a genuine apology without fear of retribution from customers, employees, or lawyers. They are able to suspend the fear, the cynicism, and say the words: "We're sorry."

Clarity of purpose enables a company to know with speed and decisiveness what actions must be taken to get the balance back when a customer situation throws things out of whack. Without clarity, a hollow apology might be thought to suffice.

Being real enables the actions to be heartfelt, genuine, and personalized. When the right tenor throughout the customer relationship already exists, an empathetic and heartfelt apology is a natural part of the conversation during the occasional failure.

Operating and making decisions to **be there** for customers on their terms enables companies to have early warning signs in place. They know when things go off track. They proactively plan actions and accountability that click into place and have thought ahead about what incidents are most common and how they will be handled.

Southwest Airlines **says "sorry"** proactively to its customers every day. Each morning, a group assembles for a meeting they call "MOM" (Morning Overview Meeting). This affectionate name is not an accident. The brainchild of Colleen Barrett, president emeritus and chief evangelist for what Southwest calls Customer LUV, the purpose of the MOM meeting is to learn about the experience you just had as a passenger of Southwest Airlines. Every morning's meeting is a review of the previous day's operation, not from Southwest's point of view, but from the passengers' point of view. Southwest wants to know what customers have gone through on their flights, with service, weather, or delays BEFORE customers contact them.

> **"A thoughtful and well-executed apology focuses on restoring and preserving the relationship."**

Let's say you just landed. The flight experience started out grandly but quickly soured. Checking in for your flight was pleasant, you found the seat you wanted, and ate your free peanuts. But there were delays taking off. Then weather in Chicago and a missed connection. You finally set foot into your home after two in the morning. The next day a letter from Southwest Airlines arrives . . . with a humble apology, a contrite and genuine explanation, a promise to improve, and a gesture to make it up to you. You had just begun thinking about how to voice your frustration when you open the letter which

stops you dead in your tracks . . . with amazement . . . with apprecia-
tion. Some customers who have experienced this even say . . . with
glee.

Who sent that letter? Surely it's some machine-generated form
letter, you might be thinking. Not a chance. What you've received is
a personal missive crafted by a member of Southwest's Proactive
Customer Service Communications Team. Any thought of changing
carriers quickly vanishes from the customer's mind. "I LOVE Southwest!" is what takes its place. Magic.

Being proactive with an apology and a resolution for bad experiences is good business for Southwest. Their swift communication,
human and contrite mea culpa, and promise to do better, paired with
an olive branch commensurate with the disruption to their customers' lives, generated a net return of $1.8 million in repeat and addi-
tional flights booked by customers who received one of their Proactive Customer Service apologies in 2007. The sales force that Southwest
Airlines creates in the 50,000 customers they amaze every year with
these gestures has a return on investment that far exceeds the number of family members, friends, and colleagues who they compel to
try this airline with the human touch.

The apology peace process is also beginning to be delivered
in groundbreaking ways in the healthcare industry. After years of
asking doctors, nurses, and other healthcare professionals to avoid
apologizing to patients for fear of malpractice suits, this industry is
learning to suspend its fear and cynicism. Withholding an explanation and apology to patients and/or families is being replaced with
empathetic and open communication. With counterintuitive, non-
zero-sum results. Nobody loses.

This change has been spearheaded largely through the efforts of a
coalition called Sorry Works!, which was founded by Doug Wojcieszak
after his family lost his oldest brother due to medical errors. Following
their personal tragedy, what Wojcieszak and his family really wanted
was a human connection, to feel some caring for what they went
through. They sought an apology and an open explanation about what
happened. But when that did not materialize; the Wojcieszak family

took their less preferable legal route, suing the hospital and doctors to get answers. Out of his personal experience, to urge healthcare providers to rethink their prevailing noncompassionate approach, Wojcieszak began the Sorry Works! coalition.

Sorry Works! fosters a process which, rather than increasing malpractice suits, encourages transparency, a swift and caring explanation and, when appropriate, a heartfelt apology for patients and their families. The Sorry Works! process establishes middle ground where fewer lawsuits occur for doctors and no constitutional infringements occur for patients and lawyers. The open communication that results yields a reduction in medical errors, as true empathetic and compassionate listening and conversation take the place of legal protocol.

It's Good Business to Say "I'm Sorry" Well.

One early adopter of Sorry Works!, the University of Michigan Hospital has experienced a steady decline in its claims and pending lawsuits after five years using the "Sorry Works!" process. From 262 claims in August 2001, the number dropped to 104 in 2006, the last figures publicly reported. Its average legal expense dropped by 50 percent, from $48,000 in 1997 to $21,000 in 2003. And case processing time shrank from 20.7 months to 9.5 months.

Other industries besides healthcare also benefit when they adopt a mind-set for apologizing sincerely and proactively. When companies and customers are able to shelve litigious approaches for straight talk and caring, surprising results occur. In the ultimate zero-sum game of "winner takes it all," companies and customers who previously fought it out in court much prefer to talk about it over coffee. Aaron Lazare, author of *On Apology*, says, "The apology is a powerful and constructive form of conflict resolution, embedded, in modified form, in religion and the judicial system. It is a method of social hearing that has grown in importance as our way of living together on our planet undergoes radical change." Moral of the story: a good apology trumps the legal system. As long as the apology is sincere and the effort to make amends is genuine. People prefer the human connection of the apology. The closure is more complete when genuine remorse and an effort to do the right thing is delivered. Back to the Golden Rule we go.

"A good apology trumps the legal system. As long as the apology is sincere and the effort to make amends is genuine."

One industry we might not think about as being potentially litigious is the lawnmower industry. If a lawn mower is not used correctly, the user can seriously injure him- or herself. And there are also times when the product can fail. The people at the Toro Company, which manufactures lawn mowers, say "I'm sorry" to customers who have been injured while using their products, regardless of who is at fault. They are truly sorry that the customer got hurt while using their product and they open the customer conversation with that. From there, the relationship shifts from "wronged customer" to two people talking about what happened. After making sure that the customer is okay and cared for, Toro finds that the conversations often shift to "How dumb was that to let the mower get close to my leg" and "Tell us about how the product could have performed better?" As a result of its proactive decision and these actions, Toro hasn't been to trial since 1994. Toro has ceased litigating suits. Rather than starting with lawyers when someone puts in a claim, they begin with caring conversation. Ninety-five percent of its cases are settled on the day of mediation or shortly thereafter. "But that's not the aim," says Andrew Byers, senior manager, corporate product integrity for Toro, based in Bloomington, Minnesota. "Often these people just want to be heard." By connecting humanity to a process previously riddled with legal requirements executed as tasks, Toro has prospered both financially and culturally.

Saying sorry well in most cases should not require a committee, consortium, or legal review. Most apologies should occur spontaneously, the moment the company knows a problem occurred. And the person who first hears the news should be in a position to respond appropriately. Both Lands' End's and L.L. Bean's guarantees free their frontline people to do the right thing. They are trusted to take action, using their own best judgment, to deliver a response warranted by the situation. There is no debating their ability to deliver a genuine apology and offer customer recovery for something that doesn't measure up.

In 1988 it was decided that the cover of the Lands' End catalog would be dedicated to the purpose of admitting to customers that, like them, people who make clothing have good days and bad days. Human hands cut the cloth. Raw materials grow inconsistently. People, not machines, sew the garments or stitch the shoes and luggage. It was a proactive olive branch admitting in advance that sometimes mistakes happen, but that if you bought from Lands' End, we would always take care of you if you received something not up to our usual standards. It reinforced our unconditional guarantee to give customers peace of mind that when those uncommon missteps occurred, we'd make it right for them on their terms. The final words in this message were:

> An electric knife cuts the fabric, but a human hand usually guides the knife. Sewing machine operators are also very human, and like each of us, they have good days and bad days.... We make progress, but still don't achieve perfection because of the imperfect nature of the beast. Things do occasionally get out to you that shouldn't, which is why we back everything with one unqualified guarantee: Guaranteed. Period.®

That message humanized Lands' End. Our explanation and the security blanket of the guarantee bonded us closer with customers. And it gave the front line what they needed to rescue customers when the company faltered from time to time.

The front line can become the hero of somebody's day in a minute—if they have been freed to do the right thing. Beloved companies give the people interacting directly with customers the ability to apologize and respond immediately when irregularities occur. In our everyday life—as we shop at the grocery store, stay in a hotel, or pick up our dry cleaning—service failures will occur. It takes so little to bring someone back around. A little bit of thinking ahead can put you and the front line in the position to recover from customer disappointment.

Certainly beyond that, there are operational blunders that occur where widespread failures impact volumes of customers. Beloved companies like Southwest Airlines review their operations every day to know the issues, resolve them, and reach out to affected customers. They identify and work out problems while they are happening. They don't wait to hear from customers—early indicators are in place.

At the end of the day, the apology really is a humanity litmus test. These are the moments when the outside world gets to see what companies (and the people inside them) are made of. It confirms to their customers that they made a good decision putting faith in them.

Learn the Story of How You Say "Sorry."

I can admit to you that finding a set of apologies to learn from was a more difficult task than I could have imagined. Perhaps it is because the best apologies remain between customers and the companies they love. Great apologies are delivered with humility. Creating fanfare around them is not in the spirit of a beloved company. And in fact, the following profiled decisions weren't trumped up and announced to the world by those who made them. Their stories were told initially by the recipients of these apologies—customers who were grateful, moved, and amazed by the gesture.

The delivery of products and services—and in many cases, the creation of them—is a human activity. And because we are human, we have good days and bad days. Customers get that more than companies give them credit for. We're all human. When things escalate, it's often because the blunders seem to be purposefully swept under the rug, and a company doesn't genuinely apologize and work to make things better.

What follows is the deconstruction of a set of decisions made by companies and by individuals inside companies who have found a way to say sorry well. The businesses range in size from relatively small to extremely large. Among them, all three categories of customer disappointment are represented: operational breakdowns, service blunders, and widespread tragedies or missteps. In each of these cases, the company prospered because it could say sorry well. When you say sorry well, you too will prosper, not only from how your actions bring customers back into your fold, but also in what your ability to apologize does for the energy inside your company.

Beloved companies don't consider the job done until the emotional connection with customers is restored. Why do they decide to apologize in this manner? Because it's the right thing to do. Our moms told us that when you hurt someone, intentionally or not, you apologize and you mean it. You right the wrong. You make peace.

To quote Nicholas Tavuchis, from his book *Mea Culpa: A Sociology of Apology and Reconciliation*, "An Apology, no matter how sincere or effective, does not and cannot undo what has been done. And yet, in a mysterious way and according to its own logic, this is precisely what it manages to do." Do you have the courage? Are you doing the apology well?

The Decision Is Yours.

Johnson & Johnson Decided to "Protect the People."

DECISION INTENT:
Protect the People.

In a 72-hour period, starting September 29, 1982, seven people died in the Chicagoland area after taking cyanide-laced capsules of Extra-Strength Tylenol, the painkiller that was the drug maker's best-selling product. Even though Johnson & Johnson was not responsible for the product tampering, they took full responsibility in acting decisively and swiftly. Their first order of business was to decide, "How do we protect the people?"

MOTIVATION: Live to the Johnson & Johnson Credo and Values.

It took Johnson & Johnson's board 20 minutes to decide how they would react to this catastrophe. With the Golden Rule firmly strapped to their back, they set to work. A product recall amounting to an estimated 31 million bottles (worth over $100 million in sales) began immediately. Advertising was halted. With bullhorns blaring, Chicago health and law-enforcement officials swarmed Chicago-area streets, warning everyone not to take Extra-Strength Tylenol capsules and to bring in suspicious bottles for testing. To prevent any more people from taking the tampered Tylenol capsules, Tylenol representatives worked with local authorities, schools, even Boy Scout troops. Children were sent home from school with notes, and transit system workers formed a continuous human megaphone, spreading the word. Anticyanide kits were distributed to all paramedic units. Telephone drives run by the Boy Scouts and church and civic groups sent folks door-to-door to reach those who might have missed the warnings.

IMPACT: Only Two Months Later, Tylenol Was Welcomed Back to the Market.

Johnson & Johnson remains the beacon for apologizing well. Because they acted swiftly and decisively from their core values, an incident that could have put the company under ultimately raised them up. Many predicted that the Tylenol brand, which accounted for 17 percent of the company's net income in 1981, would never recover from the sabotage. As expected, Tylenol's marketplace share dropped to 7 percent in September 1982. Only two months later, Tylenol headed back to the market, with gelcaps and caplets and extensive safety precautions in packaging and labeling. By February 1983 market share grew to 28 percent. Since then, Tylenol gelcaps have recaptured 92 percent of the capsule segment sales lost after the cyanide incident. Would you pass the "Tylenol Test" in a crisis situation? Would your first reaction be to take care of customers, or would you consider your options more carefully to determine what you *had* to do to mitigate harm and liability?

What's Your
REACTION
TIME
in a
CUSTOMER
CRISIS?

What's your timeline for taking care of customers when the unthinkable happens?

Are there plans you can set in motion as soon as a crisis occurs?

Are you ready?

Decide to SAY SORRY.

Netflix Decided
That Honesty Is the Best Recovery.

DECISION INTENT: Prepare All Customers, Not Just Those Impacted.

Netflix, the DVD-by-mail service with 10 million subscribers experienced a severe technology glitch in August 2008 that interrupted and halted shipping of DVDs to subscribers. Netflix confessed immediately on their Web site, saying, "IMPORTANT: Your DVD Shipments Have Likely Been Delayed." They didn't sweep the problem under the rug and didn't try to hide from the blame. Netflix followed up with e-mails to make sure all customers heard the news. Not all customers even knew that there was a delay. Didn't matter. Netflix was honest in telling everyone and swift in extending an olive branch, automatically applying a credit to subscribers' next billing statements. New Netflix subscribers who had their first shipments delayed received this message, "We recognize that this is not a good way to begin your Netflix membership and we'll automatically extend your free trial."

MOTIVATION: Service Is Required to Stay Relevant in Customers' Lives.

In 1999, Netflix introduced what was then a landmark product when they began offering DVD rentals by mail. Prior to that, we all trudged to the video store for rentals. Netflix gave consumers an option to go online, make selections, read reviews, and get the DVDs for viewing via their mailboxes. Service and "delight-ing" customers has been the backbone of the company's offering, and service has fueled their growth. As the market has changed, and Netflix's easy delivery method has faced heavy competition from digital delivery services such as iTunes and the Comcast cable box, they continued to differentiate with service. So, when this glitch occurred, Netflix knew they needed to recover quickly, honestly, and in their own unique way to prove that they were worthy of having customers stick around.

IMPACT: 85 Percent of New Customers Were Convinced to Sign Up by Existing Customers.

Netflix's "End of Week" blog update after the shipping debacle posted the message. "Apologies to all once again and thanks for hanging in there with us." A customer responded with: "Forget all those whiney haters. You guys did your best. You deserve praise for getting through it, not hatred for having some hiccups." It's estimated that Netflix's recovery cost it $6 million. Because they communicated directly with customers, their decision and actions are being applauded and fueling their growth. Ninety-three percent of existing subscribers say they "talk up" how great Netflix is to everyone they know. In 2008, the average cost to acquire a new subscriber was reduced by 23 percent. Revenue grew 19 percent and profit increased 45 percent. How about you? Would you so readily fess up to an issue not all customers are even aware of?

Do you confess to *customers* WHEN *something happens?*

The companies who are upfront and let all customers know when something goes wrong prepare everyone for a better experience.

They show their true colors.

Decide to SAY SORRY.

Nurse Next Door Decided to Send Humble Pies.

DECISION INTENT: Apologize, Fix the Problem, Be Humble.

As Catherine Walker's Alzheimer's disease advanced, her daughter Gail Watson tried to both balance her mother's disease and care for her ailing father. Struggling as caregiver to both her parents, she found Nurse Next Door, a company that rescues caregivers by providing support to help care for loved ones at home. Founded in 2001 by John DeHart and Ken Sim, Nurse Next Door was born out of their personal experiences when their caregiver search caused concern as they were repeatedly sent inappropriate candidates. Sim and DeHart built a business that has grown rapidly, but as any fast-growing business knows, growing pains occur. So they decided that when mistakes happen, they would send a sincere and heartfelt apology, explaining what went wrong, how they'd resolve the situation, and humbly asking forgiveness.

MOTIVATION: Earn the Right Back to Customers' Trust.

When they slip up, Nurse Next Door sends a freshly baked pie as part of their apology. Not any old pie—they send a HUMBLE PIE, with a note that says, "We are very humbled by our mistake and sincerely apologize for the poor service." They depend on a few local bakers in Vancouver to supply the pies, the most notable of which is an outfit called Acme Humble Pie. Sim and DeHart say, "What's wrong with eating a little humble pie?" Especially when a customer is at stake?

IMPACT: Spent $1,500 on Humble Pies. Saved $100,000 in Business.

Gail Watson received one of those pies after Nurse Next Door missed her initial appointment. Though she was angry at first, the swift delivery of a heartfelt apology and the whimsy and humility of this simple gesture took the edge off. Ms. Watson remains a loyal customer today. What started as a spontaneous gesture by one employee is now a regular part of how Nurse Next Door nurses customers' wounds from the occasional service failure. DeHart estimates that in 2008 Nurse Next Door spent $1,500 on humble pies, but saved about $100,000 in sales. In just over five years, Nurse Next Door has grown to become British Columbia's largest home healthcare company. "It's more about keeping clients than a question of whose fault it is. The value of lost clients is very high," DeHart says. "And satisfied customers share their experience with friends and family." Nurse Next Door thrived in 2008, experiencing an increase in client growth over 25 percent. It's likely that their much-talked-about services fuel their growth . . . or do people just want a piece of that pie? What's your version of "humble pie"? Are you open enough to consider that there are times when you'll need one, and proactively go out there and find a baker to make them?

Is Your Humility Oven Lit?

Can you bake a humble pie?

Acknowledging a mistake shows that you're human. Admitting it is hard. But it's what customers crave. Do you have the DNA to say "Sorry" and mean it?

Decide to SAY SORRY.

Greg from Zane's Cycles Decided to Volunteer a Week of His Pay to Save a Customer.

DECISION INTENT: A Genuine Act of Contrition.

A very special bike was to be placed in the window of Zane's Cycles bike shop on Valentine's Day so a wife could show her husband the bike she was buying for him. Because it was on layaway, the plan was for her and her spouse to go to dinner and pass the store on the way there. But Greg, one of the salespeople at Zane's, forgot to put the bike in the window. Zane's had lost the trust of a customer. To apologize, the next day, the bike was delivered to the home of the customer and Zane's forgave the amount not yet paid. It also proffered a gift certificate for dinner to re-create the deflated Valentine's Day event, and arranged for a catered lunch for the business colleagues who had taken the time to be standing there at the window to see the surprise. After this expression of humility and an apology, Zane's was forgiven. But what about Greg, who had forgotten to put the bike in the window? Chris Zane received an apology letter with a check enclosed (which he never cashed) for half of the cost of the bike. Greg was completely willing to be out a week's pay to right the wrong.

MOTIVATION: Live Up to What Zane's Stands For.

Because Greg knew that Zane's valued each customer's lifetime value, he took responsibility for his action.

He was humble. He fessed up and he took it on the chin. His motivation was to live up to what Zane's stood for. And he did. Zane's knew that they had lost a moment in time for that customer and decided to make up that moment and repair the severed trust. Greg decided to make it up to Zane's.

IMPACT: Zane's Culture Stuck When It Was Most Important.

The "Valentine's Day customer" got a bike for her husband and MANY accessories. But Greg, the employee, is the real key to this story. His actions prove that what Zane's has is real. The culture stuck when it was most important—throughout decision making under duress. This is because Greg works in an environment where he is encouraged to do the right thing. The recovery of this one customer, while memorable, is not an isolated incident in which heroic actions were taken that did not require any management review or consideration. The natural instinct at Zane's is to do the right thing—to make the customer whole, to repair the relationship. And to do it with genuine care, regret, and humility. (Greg is still a valued team member at Zane's Cycles.)

Does Your Culture Stick

When Times Are Tough?

When things go wrong and a decision needs to be made about how to right the wrong, is this your shining moment?

Do company values kick in to provide direction? Are people clear on how to do what's right? Do they have permission?

Decide to SAY SORRY.

Intuit Decided
on a $15 Million Apology for Their TurboTax Errors in 2007.

DECISION INTENT: Remove the Panic, Fix the Problem, and Eliminate Customer Penalties.
It's April 15, and you take the last few minutes before the 12 midnight deadline to review your tax return before filing it electronically through TurboTax, run by Intuit. Then you click "submit" and the unthinkable happens. Your computer screen flashes: "Servers overloaded, try again in 2 hours." Terror sets in. Your only hope is that you'll receive understanding about your predicament . . . from the IRS! This is the account of a blogger, who told her story to the world on the Internet. In total, 200,000 customers were unable to e-file their TurboTax returns on time in 2007. They needn't have worried. Within one day, Intuit had apologized to customers affected by the slowdown in the company's electronic filing process and removed their worry about having to explain to the IRS. Intuit acted decisively, humanely, and in their customers' best interest. They saved the day for their customers.

MOTIVATION: Don't Make Customers Pay for Our Mistake.
This message from President Steve Bennett set Intuit's tone and their course of action: "We deeply regret the frustration and anxiety this caused our customers. This is not the experience customers have come to expect from Intuit. It's not acceptable to us, and we will do right by our customers who were impacted by this delay." Intuit secured a concession from the IRS allowing taxpayer customers affected by the delay to file their returns until midnight on April 19 without penalty, and committed to pay any other penalties customers incurred as a result of the delay. TurboTax customers received automatic refunds of credit card charges made during the period of time when the servers overloaded.

IMPACT: 81 Percent of Sales Are Attributable to Word of Mouth.
Intuit invested $15 million on this action. Decisions and actions like these drive Intuit's growth. Most customers' sentiments echoed those of the blogger who said: "Intuit has blown me away." Brad Smith, Intuit's CEO, attributes 81 percent of sales directly to customers telling other customers about the company. Even during slow economic times, Intuit revenues grew, increasing 11 percent in the last quarter of 2008 to $478 million. In moments of service failure, customers see a company's character. Beloved companies put as much forethought into planning customer-experience recovery as they do planning recovery for IT and natural disasters. How many 12-hour clocks would wind down before your company responded to a customer problem? Customers are watching the clock—every minute. The amount of time that goes by before you respond tells them the story of how much you care.

Do you **accept** accountability?

When things go wrong, customers see what you're made of.

When mistakes occur, do you act decisively and in their best interest?

Do your "rescue" plans show a commitment to make customers whole, or just to get past the incident?

Decide to SAY SORRY.

Dr. Tapas K. Das Gupta Decided
to Personally Apologize to His Patient.

DECISION INTENT: Freely Admit His Mistake and Apologize.

Dr. Tapas K. Das Gupta has seen a great deal in his experience as chairman of surgical oncology at the University of Illinois Medical Center in Chicago. So when he saw his patient's X-ray, he immediately saw the mistake he made. Dr. Das Gupta had been operating on cancer patients for 40 years when he accidentally removed the wrong sliver of tissue from his patient. Instead of taking a segment from the ninth rib, he removed it from the eighth rib. And he knew what he had to do. He personally met with his patient and her husband to extend his deep apology. Without any excuse, with humility and remorse, he said, "After all these years, I cannot give you any excuse whatsoever. It is just one of those things that occurred. I have to some extent harmed you."

MOTIVATION Dr. Das Gupta's Only Motivation Was to Ease the Family's Suffering.

For Dr. Das Gupta, extending this compassionate apology was his natural response. His actions were reinforced because he worked within a healthcare system, the University of Illinois Medical Center in Chicago, which encourages doctors to voluntarily disclose medical errors with a sincere apology, explanation, and plan to resolve what occurred. These medical professionals are trained in how to respond with patients when things don't go as planned. Dr.

Timothy B. McDonald, chief safety and risk officer for the University of Illinois, says that "errors should become teaching opportunities rather than badges of shame: I think this is the key to patient safety in this country. If you do this with a transparent point of view, you're more likely to figure out what's wrong and put processes in place to improve it."

IMPACT: Care and Forgiveness Trump Anger. Malpractice Filings Dropped by Half.

Dr. Das Gupta's patient felt that he was sincere in his explanation and desire to help her. She did not sue either her physician or the University of Illinois Medical Center; instead they reached a small settlement out of court. She explained to her lawyer that "the doctor was so completely candid, completely honest, and so frank that she and her husband—usually it's the husband who wants to pound the guy—[found] that all the anger was gone." Since the University of Illinois Medical Center began its program to openly and honestly discuss errors, deliver a sincere apology, and plan for assisting patients and their families, it has seen the number of malpractice filings drop by half. They have acknowledged a preventable error and apologized in 37 cases. Only one patient has sued.

Can you suspend *the fear* and say "we're sorry"?

Are you able to table the "corporate" response and deliver one that connects on a personal level? **Can you suspend the fear and talk openly and honestly with your customers?**

Decide to SAY SORRY.

Southwest Airlines Decided
to Proactively Apologize to Customers.

DECISION INTENT: Apologize Even Before Customers Complain.
Colleen Barrett, president emeritus of Southwest Airlines, told me, "We knew from day one that we wanted to be in the customer service business. The business we were in just happened to provide airline transportation." Colleen's notion is this: if you want to be best in customer service, then you've got to be proactive about it. You can't wait for customers to tell you about your problems. You've got to be out ahead of them every day. And that includes when you make a mistake. So Colleen established a manifesto and a group dedicated to what Southwest calls "Proactive Customer Service." This gets right to the heart of the matter for why this team exists.

MOTIVATION: Southwest's Desire to "Wow."
Southwest has turned the process for "saying sorry" into a core competency of their business. Each morning, a "MOM" (Morning Overview Meeting) is convened. The people who run the airline's operations, its meteorologist, and Proactive Customer Service team members review the flights of the previous day for delays, issues, and service glitches. They get a read on the weather for that day that might have brought passenger delays and challenges to airports. Then the Proactive Customer Service team goes to work. They imagine themselves as passengers and decide which events warrant an apology, a hand of

human kindness from Southwest. Depending on the severity of the situation, this ranges from offering the passengers' next flight for free to a percentage off in the form of a LUV voucher. All come with a hand-signed, personalized letter customized to the experience customers encountered. No mass produced "sorry" letter allowed here!

IMPACT: Proactive Apologies Generated a Net Return of $1.8 Million in 2007.
For Southwest, their instinct to take "Golden Rule behaviors" makes them profitable. It helps to keep them flying. Based on how Southwest Airlines customers redeemed their LUV vouchers, and after completing the appropriate revenue accounting practices, a net return of $1.8 million was generated in repeat flying in 2007 by customers who received letters sent from the PCS team. Southwest Airlines has consistently received the lowest ratio of complaints per passenger boarded of all major U.S. carriers that have been reporting their statistics to the Department of Transportation since September 1987. The *Wall Street Journal* named Southwest Airlines the airline champ of 2007. In a 2008 TIME.com survey, Southwest Airlines ranked number one for being the friendliest airline. Can you form a proactive team to do what Southwest does?

How
Proactive
Are
You?

Do you have a proactive recovery plan for knowing what your customers experience? When something goes wrong, what actions are set in motion?

Does your recovery "wow" your customers?

Decide to SAY SORRY.

L.L. Bean Decided
to Help the Front Line Right the "Wrong."

DECISION INTENT: Give Customers Peace of Mind.

Alma Rettew bought a holiday gift for a friend, and asked L.L. Bean, whom she bought it from, to get it to her friend on a specific date (the company has a service to do this). Unfortunately, there was a glitch in the system, and the gift arrived before the holiday, spoiling Alma's surprise for her friend. When Alma called in to L.L. Bean to register her complaint, her fear and "dukes up" concern that she might have to fight to get her situation addressed was quickly disarmed by the quick and rapid response she received. Ms. Rettew was offered two options for solving her problem. She could receive a refund, or have a complimentary duplicate of her gift sent to her recipient at the correct time. In addition, she received a sincere apology and a promise that the company would contact her friend and explain what had transpired. The burden would fall on L.L. Bean, not her, to make things right with her friend. After all, it was their mistake, and they were accountable. All corrective actions were successfully completed. And while this solution was probably an unusual experience for Ms. Rettew, it is not an uncommon occurrence at L.L. Bean.

MOTIVATION: Free Phone Reps to Do the Right Thing.

The L.L. Bean guarantee gives customers peace of mind, it frees the company's front line to do the right thing, and it keeps them close to their small-town company culture. "Sell good merchandise at a reasonable profit; treat your customers like human beings and they'll always come back for more," Leon Leonwood Bean said in 1912 when he founded the company. It remains true today. Bean also said, "A lot of people have fancy things to say about Customer Service, but it's just a day-in, day-out, ongoing, never-ending, persevering, compassionate kind of activity."

IMPACT: L.L. Bean Enjoys Annual Sales of $1.5 Billion.

L.L. Bean has sustained their respect for customers and the front line throughout the entire history of the company. From a one-man operation to its place as a global organization with sales of $1.5 billion today, the company has grown by honoring its customers—and by honoring the employees who serve customers by giving them the trust and the tools to do what's right. L.L. Bean is ranked the number one "Online Leader" by *Women's Wear Daily* (in its 2008 Top 100 Online Retail Satisfaction Index Report). *BusinessWeek* magazine named L.L. Bean as one of its top 25 service "champs" in 2008 and 2009. In 2008, for the sixth consecutive year, L.L. Bean ranks first among clothing catalog companies in the Brand Keys Customer Loyalty Index.

Can your front line RESCUE customers?

When an unhappy customer calls, does your front line have "permission" to do the right thing?

Frontline people who think on their feet for customers in distress sets beloved companies apart.

Where are you in nurturing this ability?

Decide to SAY SORRY.

Baxter CEO Harry Kraemer Jr. Decided to Voluntarily Reduce His Bonus

DECISION INTENT: Act Immediately Regardless of Who Is at Fault.

"Let's make sure we do the right thing," CEO Harry Kraemer told Alan Heller, president of the Baxter International Inc. division responsible for dialysis equipment, when dialysis patient deaths began in August 2001 in Madrid, Spain, and Croatia. Rather than waiting to know if they were at fault, Baxter took accountability immediately, with a global recall of all of the filters and a hold on distribution of warehoused filters. It was finally determined that a fluid made by another company that was not flushed out of some of the filters during equipment testing had entered patients' bloodstreams during dialysis, causing the deaths. Even though this error was not caused by Baxter, their equipment was involved. CEO Kraemer didn't blame other parties and didn't hide the facts. He apologized publicly with heartfelt empathy and humility. As a result, Baxter decided to shut down the plants that made the filters. They settled with all families involved.

MOTIVATION: Decide and Act Guided by Values.

"What we try to do is do the right thing," Kraemer said when asked about this situation. "I think there's a tendency to make things more complex than they are. If we live the values we profess, we'll add shareholder value. I don't see a conflict."

Under his watch, Kraemer made sure that Baxter could live those values by opening up dialogue on translating values to decision making. The company's actions related to this incident cost Baxter $189 million. Holding himself personally accountable, Kraemer asked the board to reduce his 2001 bonus by 40 percent. And he recommended that accountable executives' bonuses should also be reduced by 20 percent.

IMPACT: Henry Kraemer Gave an Indelible Lesson on Deciding with Your Values.

As a result of Baxter International's 2001 filter crisis, the stock dropped, but it soon recovered. The financial community applauded the straightforward talk and recovery. And Baxter's employees got a lesson. The congruence between values and decisions even in a tragedy buoyed employees' faith in Baxter and Kraemer. Henry Kraemer was flooded with e-mails and messages from proud employees. Kraemer said in an interview one year after the incident. "If the values are authentic, then so are the decisions and the actions." In a time of crisis, are these your proudest moments? The decisions will be tough, but making the right ones will signal your values, what you believe in, and if your decisions are guided by them.

Do You **Learn** and **Change** *From Your Mistakes?*

Remorse is great.

But change means you took your customers' experience to heart.

Companies customers love make lasting change so no other customers experience what went wrong.

Decide to SAY SORRY.

How Well Do You Say "Sorry"?

When things go wrong, are you nimble enough to spring into action, identify the issue, plan a recovery, and implement it within a day? How about within hours? That's what your customers expect and deserve.

It has been proven that a genuine apology strengthens the emotional connection that a customer has with a company. Being human and prone to making mistakes, we're in luck. We have the opportunity regularly to make amends.

"Being human and prone to making mistakes, we're in luck.

"We have the opportunity regularly to make amends."

I'll end this chapter with an infamous human dispute that occurred between not a company and a customer, but between two sports legends. George Steinbrenner, owner of the New York Yankees, unceremoniously dumped beloved Yogi Berra as manager of the team in the middle of the 1985 season. Steinbrenner didn't deliver the news personally. He jobbed out the task to a member of his organization. Steinbrenner never apologized to Yogi Berra for his action or the manner in which he carried it out. Berra vowed never to set foot in Yankee Stadium again. Many secondhand invitations to return to Yankee Stadium were delivered to Berra over the years, but he didn't budge until Steinbrenner got personally involved. Fourteen years later, Steinbrenner finally apologized to Yogi Berra. This belated apology violated the first principle of a good apology: swift delivery. But it was sincere and humane, and he took the blame for the action. After 14 years, they made amends.

Apologies to customers are being tossed about very freely these days. But they often are missing the components which give an apology meaning. Yogi Berra knew when Steinbrenner was finally *genuine* about making amends. And only then did he agree to accept his apology. He could tell that Steinbrenner had had a change of heart.

Repairing the emotional connection with your customers and reaping good results has conditions. Your apology must:

- Be genuine.
- Restore confidence in being associated with you.
- Honor those harmed.
- Explain and work to resolve the problem.
- Be delivered swiftly and with humility.

Remember when you were a kid and your brother or sister punched you or pinched you? Sure, he or she apologized. But it didn't mean much because (a) your parent was usually prompting the words, and (b) you'd been apologized to many times before, just to be punched again another day. This is what we put our customers through when we deliver a hollow apology and then don't fix the problem causing the issue. You'll likely get credit when you apologize once for a problem. But when it repeats, another letter for the same problem won't cut it. Your currency with customers and their trust in you will dwindle.

> "Remember when you were a kid and your brother or sister punched you?
>
> "Sure, he or she apologized. But it didn't mean much."

Beloved companies turn "recovery" into an opportunity that says to customers "Who else would respond this way?" They are zealots about recovering customer goodwill. The measure of the company is determined in these moments. And they obsess over every moment of these situations because they know that customers are keeping score.

Do you deliver "Sorry" well?

When You Apologize...

Are you genuine?

Do you restore confidence in being associated with you?

Do you honor those impacted and resolve their problem?

Do you deliver your apology swiftly and with humility?

The beloved companies turn "recovery" into an opportunity that says to customers "Who else would respond this way?" When things go wrong, do these conditions exist for repairing the emotional connection with your customers?

What's Your Story:
How Do You Say "Sorry"?

Simplicity. Open communication of values. Respect, responsiveness, results. Over and over and over again. If the values are authentic, then so are the decisions and the actions.

—Retired Baxter
CEO Henry Kraemer

For a tool kit on how to use these questions to improve your business, go to www.customerbliss.com

7

The Decision
Is YOURS

**Whenever you see a successful business,
someone once made a courageous decision.**

—PETER DRUCKER

Throughout this book, you've been invited to consider the story that the collective decisions of your organization tells customers, employees, and the marketplace. You've seen examples of decisions made by beloved companies of all sizes and how they impact their customers and employees. And you've been provided with questions so that you can reflect on what message you are sending through your decision making.

As you progressed through each chapter, learning about the beloved companies, understanding their decisions, and contrasting them to your own, you should now know how different or similar your decisions are to theirs. And how your results compare.

Are Customers Telling Your Story?

What story is emerging about who you are and what you value? Are your decisions reflecting what you intended? Do they indicate to employees and customers how much you honor them? When you make decisions that respect and honor customers you will earn their respect—eventually their love. Are your decisions compelling customers to tell others to try your products and services? Are customers telling your story?

In this final chapter, to help you understand how your decisions impact your customer and employee relationships, all of the questions posed throughout this book are assembled in one place. You can work through these questions with your organization to diagnose the strength of your current relationships. Your collective answers will tell you how you are seen from the outside looking in. They will tell the story of who you are and what you value based on the decisions you make to run your business. For a tool kit on how to use these questions throughout your organization, please go to www.customer bliss.com.

The Story of Our Decisions:
What They Say About Who We Are and What We Value.

Decision 1: Do We Decide to Believe?

"We trust our customers. We trust those who serve them."

Inside the beloved companies, they decide to believe. Trust and belief are cornerstones of their relationships. By deciding to trust customers, they are freed from extra rules, policies, and layers of bureaucracy that create a barrier between them and their customers. And by deciding to believe that employees can and will do the right thing, second-guessing, reviewing every action, and the diminishing of employees' abilities to think on their feet are replaced with shared energy, ideas, and a desire to stick around.

Are We Transparent with Our Customers?

When Griffin Hospital decided to open up records to customers and their families, their trust was reciprocated in greater relationships and reduced malpractice incidents.

- What information are we holding close to our vest because it gives us power over customers?
- Is there anything we know that customers could prosper from knowing and understanding?
- Do we believe trust is reciprocated?

Do We Fan the Flames of Trust?

The Container Store decided that all employees should know their sensitive financial information. Sharing information guides employees and elevates their purpose.

- What actions can we take, or policies can we remove to show employees we believe in them?
- How can we decide to honor the intelligence of employees?
- Can we "skinny down" our rule book?

Do We Practice Democratic Decision Making?

W.L. Gore continues to innovate by shedding formal hierarchy in favor of the power of the idea. Belief that good ideas come from everyone is their growth engine.

- Do the best ideas of our company get to see the light of day?
- Are good ideas given a chance to prosper, no matter where they come from?

Do We Believe Customers Are an Asset or a Cost Center?

Zane's Cycles doesn't take collateral from customers who test ride its bikes. Of the 4,000 sold each year, only 5 bikes are stolen. Zane's calculates the lifetime value of a customer at $12,500. "Why start that relationship by questioning someone's integrity?" asks Chris Zane.

- Do we know the value of our customers? Does everyone in our company?
- Does how we value customers guide decision making?
- Are we investing in customers or managing costs?

What's Our Power Source for Bonding with Customers?

Trader Joe's believes in the taste buds of their people and their customers to line their shelves. Passion and personal connections bond them to customers. Detachment from customers comes when they are only defined by research and reports.

- Inside our company are we regular customers of our products and services? Do we taste our food, wear our clothes, and experience the same services we deliver to customers?
- Do we connect regularly with customers to see them use, taste, or try on our products?

Do We Dare to Bare What Our Customers Share?

CustomInk decided to put uncensored customer reviews on its Web site because they believe in the truth of their customers' words. They trust customers to guide potential customers.

- Do we trust current customers to guide future customers with their feedback?
- Do we censor customer reviews? Do we believe in the truth of our customers' words?

Is Our "Trusting Cup" Half Full or Half Empty?

Wegmans decided that no customer should leave unhappy. They trust the people serving customers in their stores to interpret what that means. Umpqua bank believes in the skills of its people to be able to shepherd customers through their entire "store" experience.

- Do we trust the majority of employees to do the right thing?
- Or do we manage to the minority?

Are We Hiring Partners or Filling Positions?

Chick-fil-A spends an extensive amount of time getting to know the values and habits of candidates so they can entrust their franchise to an operator for life.

- Do we select for lifelong values?
- Are the people who enter our business today people we want to become a part of the story of our business?

Who Has a Seat at Our Table?

Harley-Davidson established their course for success during rapid growth because they shelved the usual boundaries between management, labor unions, and workers to establish a collaborative partnership for running their operations.

- Do we involve employees in planning their destiny?
- Do we honor genuine partnership and believe in its power?
- Do we nurture a company of contributors?

Decision 2: Do We Decide with Clarity of Purpose?

"Our iron-clad integrity and clarity guides the direction of our decisions."

The companies beloved by their customers work hard every day to resist the pull of "normal" business practices to create a powerful human connection with their customers. Beloved companies take the time to be clear about what their unique promise is for their customers' lives. They use this clarity when they make decisions so they align to this purpose, to this promise. Clarity of purpose guides choices and unites the organization. It elevates people from executing tasks to delivering experiences customers will want to repeat and tell others about.

What Defines Our Experience?

When Apple began building their stores, they created the "Genius Bar" to reflect the experience of friendship and congeniality found at the bars of the Four Seasons and Ritz-Carlton hotels. This purpose gives clarity to how people act and deliver when customers "belly-up."

- When we are deciding on one action over another, is there an experience endgame that steers direction?
- Would ten random people in our company consistently describe our customer experience?

Do We Hire People Who Fit the Soul of Our Company? Do We Encourage Those Who Don't to Leave?

Zappos.com keeps screening for culture fit, all the way through a new employee's orientation. They let people opt out of their new job by offering them $2,000 for their time if the new hire believes they can't be passionate about the Zappos.com culture and job they were just hired for.

- Beloved companies are filled with people who love what they do. Is ours?
- How do we screen people during hiring to ensure that they possess our core values?
- Do we help people gracefully exit our company if they don't fit our customer culture?

Does Our Experience Have an Expiration Date?

Zane's Cycles decided to guarantee its entire customer experience so that customers feel peace of mind. This frees the front line to do the right thing, and frees them from policies, rules, and regulations regarding what they can and cannot do for customers.
- Do our service offerings put the monkey on our customers' backs to keep track of when and how they can get help from us, redeem points, or take advantage of our warranty?
- What part of our experience can we guarantee to give customers trouble-free peace of mind?

If We Shed Standard Industry Practices . . . What Could We Become?

Umpqua Bank got rid of the ropes and the lines that define banking as part of their metamorphosis from "bank" to store. They shed most standard banking practices to get rid of the feeling that banking was a chore.

- What industry habits can we remove?
- Can we make a few initial commitments to set our company apart?
- What will we commit to *never* doing? What will we commit to *always* doing?

What Are Our Customer-Experience Bookends?

Griffin Hospital decided to eliminate the fear of hospital visits with music in their parking lots and a concierge in their lobby. The memory of these experience bookends bond visitors to them.

- Do we have a purposeful beginning and ending to moments of customer contact?
- Are we creating memories or executing tasks?

How Fresh Are We?

LUSH removes one-third of its cosmetics products every year to keep customer interest high. They breed excitement for customers who keep going back to find out what's new.

- Are we fearless in dismissing the old and bringing in the new?
- How do we keep customers enticed and interested?

What's Our Vibe?

Many beloved companies have a certain energy that defines them. At Trader Joe's, employees wear Hawaiian shirts and deck out their stores in rustic décor. The kitschy environment and attitude makes it hard to take themselves too seriously.

- Do we take ourselves too seriously? Beloved companies all laugh at themselves at times.
- Beloved companies have a certain personality that marks them in their customers' memories. What's ours?

What Pushes Our "Yes" Button?

IKEA designs the price tag first because the price is a major component of the promise that it delivers to customers. Before they say "yes" to a product, they steer decisions through conditions to ensure that their low price and value promises are met.

- What steers our decisions?
- What conditions must always be met before we say "yes"?
- Do those conditions exist?

Do We Deliver a Closing Memory?

Newegg.com wanted to ensure that customers didn't see pop-up ads as the closing memory of a purchase with them. So they eliminated post-purchase pop-up ads. They don't want to cloud customers' closing experiences in the name of making a few dollars on pop-up ads.

- What's the last thing we want our customers to remember about us after they say "good-bye"?

Decision 3: Do We Decide to Be Real?

*"We have a spirited soul, humanity in our touch,
and a personality that's all ours."*

Beloved companies shed their fancy packaging and break down the barriers of "big company, little customer." The relationship is between people who share the same values and revel in each other's foibles, quirks, and spirit. And that's what draws them to each other. Beloved companies decide to create a safe place where the personality and creativity of people come through. It makes them beloved to customers who gravitate to their particular brand of humanity.

Do We Walk in Our Customers' Shoes?

Walking in the shoes of the military personnel and families they serve keeps USAA delivering the service they are known for. New hires get "orders" to their assignment and eat the "ready to eat" meals served to enlisted personnel.

- Can we describe a day in the life of our customers?
- Do we know what keeps our customers up at night?
- We need to understand their lives to serve their lives. Do we?

What's Our "White Paper Bag"?

Amy's Ice Creams in Austin, Texas, gives applicants a white paper bag that they must return with an expression of who they are. That's how they know if an applicant fits their culture. Headsets.com conducts a customer service "tryout," watching candidates on the job first.

- How do we decide who to pick as the people who will deliver our special blend of service, support, and personal connection to our customers?
- Is our interview process as unique as our business?
- Should we give applicants a "customer service tryout" like Headsets.com does?

Is Our Communication "Vanilla"?

CD Baby has created a firestorm of buzz with the whimsical order-confirmation e-mail that they send to customers. All beloved companies find a way to infuse their personality and spirit into their communications.

- Would our customers want to know us after reading our letters, our e-mails, our packing slips, or our invoices?
- How do we decide on communication to customers?
- Do we have a clear "voice" that is ours alone?

What Does Our Underbelly Say About Us?

WestJet got rid of the shorthand language that permeates the airline business and over time defines customers as inanimate objects, such as "PAX in 12B wants a coffee." They grew by trading standard airline behavior, policies, and lingo for honoring and respecting passengers.

- Behind the scenes, how do our people talk about customers?
- If someone was standing on the other side of the wall with a glass . . . what would they hear?

How Do We Stay Connected to Customers?

Southwest Airlines and Zappos.com follow customers 24 hours a day to learn about their experiences. And they communicate through Twitter in an everyman, conversational way. Customers get to know the people in these companies. There is no "corporate veneer"—just good relationships based on trust and trying to do the right thing.

- Too many companies still jump to surveys and focus groups to find out what their customers need. All they really need to do is reach out. Do we?
- Do customers feel like we are people they can talk to?
- Are we part of their lives in a natural way?

What Gets Between Us and Our Customers?

Trader Joe's knows that what separates them from other grocery stores are the moments of personal interactions with customers. They know and obsess over every one, down to ensuring that the "ping" of the checkout scanners doesn't drown out conversations.

- Do we obsess about the moments of connection? About how we relate?
- Do we think about not just what we say, but how we say it?

Do We Encourage Flexibility and Gut?

The Container Store's mantra is to be like "Gumby." This is their whimsical way of saying to all employees, "Do what it takes." It gives everyone permission to find the right solution for each situation. Put your humanity into it. Be "Gumby."

- Do we give customers a positive view of how our front line is encouraged to do what's right, to work together, and to serve customers?
- Are people encouraged to cross boundaries and work together?

How Do We Show What We're Made of?

T-shirt supplier and printer CustomInk always donates to the charities their customers are having T-shirts made for. With this one gesture they let customers know how moved they are by the work they do. It connects them on a human level with their customers.

- What selfless acts tell our customers and employees about what matters to us on a personal level?

Is Mutual Respect a Core Competency?

Headsets.com staffs for humanity. And they let people go for lack of respect. Founder Mike Faith says, "The customer deserves our respect. Sometimes they could be wrong. But they always deserve respect. If you roll your eyes or in any way don't deliver respect, you are gone."

- Are we great at finding and nurturing people who develop and earn customer respect?
- Do we have a service "tryout" for the people of our company who will represent us?

Decision 4: Do We Decide to Be There for Customers?

"We must earn the right to our continued relationship with customers."

It's an everyday charge up the hill to be there for customers in ways that are important to them. Beloved companies gladly do the hard work. They're in the scrimmage every day to earn the right for their customers to return.

Beloved companies think and rethink how to conduct themselves, so they earn the right to their customers' continued business. The "experience" they deliver is far more than the execution of an operating plan. They leave customers thinking, "Who else would have done this?" "Where else could I get this?" "I want to do this again." By creating reliability in the way they do business, and fusing that with moments of contact delivered from the customer's point of view, beloved companies earn the right to grow.

Do We Know Our Customers?

Zara works to appeal to "fashionista" customers motivated by the "hunt." They produce small batches to create exclusivity and turn over product rapidly. Customers swarm to stores to see what is new and what they must not miss.

- Does how customers go through their day inspire and inform the actions we take?
- Do we plan for how we impact our customers' lives based on how they live?

Do Customers Look Forward to Seeing Us?

"Umpqua Bank is part Internet café, part community center, and part bank. The coffee's good and it's not a bad place to sit and read a book." Umpqua's goal was to make walking into their bank something people look forward to.

- Are our operating decisions based on executing tasks?
- Or delivering an experience that complements our customers' day?
- Does our front line have the freedom to customize experiences for customers?

Have We Planned for Heroic Acts of Kindness?

Zane's Cycles decided to give away bike parts costing less than $1. This makes Zane's the lifeline for their customers throughout bicycle ownership. These gestures create "wow" memories that pull customers back to them.

- Is everyone ready to go the extra mile?
- Do they have permission? Are they inspired?
- Do we celebrate heroism every day?

Do We Accept the Order and the Responsibility?

Newegg.com takes a product off their Web site the minute that they run out of inventory. They won't mislead customers about stock and won't take customers' orders or payment for products that can't ship immediately.

- Are we as quick to fulfill orders as our customers expect and deserve?
- Do our customers always know when our products and services will be available—and when they will not?

What's Our Service Magnet?

Commerce Bank (now TD Bank) puts a penny arcade in every store. It's part of the entertainment of being there. And they don't charge a dime for it.

- What's our service magnet?
- What can we extend to connect with customers and earn the right to their business?

Can We Blur the Line between Customer and Company?

Threadless.com sells out of every product they sell because their T-shirts are designed, voted on, and bought by their customer community of over 700,000 members. Beloved companies tap the passionate energy of their customers to grow and prosper.

- Do customers have a seat at our table and a hand in the design of their experience and the products we offer?

When Our Service Providers Change . . . Do We Provide Continuity of Service?

Edward Jones focuses on client relationships by ensuring that when customers receive new advisors, there is no disruption or change in their service level. Experienced advisors mentor new advisors. Beloved companies lock customers into their corporate memory.

- Do we make customers restart their relationship when their contact people change?
- Does our service continue seamlessly when a customer's account changes hands?

Can Everyone Jump a Fence to Serve a Customer?

Rackspace teams eliminate customer "hot potatoes" and provide support from their customer's point of view. Customer support is never lost in the handoffs between silos and departments.

- Do the boundary lines of our organization chart keep people from going the extra mile?
- Is collaboration something we're good at, or do the silos impact the customer experience?
- Do people care more about where they sit or how they matter?

Is Our Experience Memorable?

Zipcar decided to go to school with college students to begin their relationship with them at a memorable time in their life. They count on the college experience to keep pulling customers back to Zipcar all throughout their life.

- Do we know the moments in our customers' lives when we can be uniquely there for them?
- Do we define our experience to deliver at the memorable moments?
- When customers look back on a time in their lives when we served them, will we be part of those memories?

Decision 5: Do We Decide to Say "Sorry"?

"We act with humility when things go wrong. We will make it right."

The humanity of a company and how it reacts in adversity shows the true colors of that company more than almost any situation they might encounter. Grace and wisdom guides the decisions of beloved companies when the chips are down—not accusations and skirting accountability. Doing the apology well is a hallmark of companies we love. It makes us love them more. How a company makes decisions to explain, react, remove the pain, and take accountability for actions signals loud and clear how they think about customers and the collective "heart" of the organization. Years of earned good intentions build up a reserve that makes forgiving the beloved companies who make sincere apologies something we're open to do.

What's Our Reaction Time in a Customer Crisis?

It took 20 minutes for Johnson & Johnson's board of directors to decide how they would "protect the people" during the Tylenol catastrophe of 1982 when seven people died in the Chicago area after taking cyanide-laced capsules of Extra-Strength Tylenol.

- What's our timeline for taking care of customers when the unthinkable happens?
- Are there plans that we can set in motion to take care of customers as soon as a crisis occurs? Are we ready?

Do We Confess to Customers When Something Happens?

Netflix, the DVD-by-mail subscription service, let all customers know that they were experiencing a technology glitch holding up requested DVD shipments. They didn't wait for customers to notice; they were proactive in admitting the error, apologizing for it, and making up for it.

- Do we openly explain to customers when something goes wrong?
- Do we wait for customers to complain or do we proactively offer a resolution for everyone?
- Which direction is the natural instinct inside our company?

Is Our Humility Oven Lit?

Home healthcare company Nurse Next Door sends out a freshly baked "humble pie" to customers when a service glitch occurs. It arrives hot and leaves a positive taste in their customers' mouths from the pie and sincerity in correcting the problem.

- Can we act with humility when things go wrong? Can we bake a humble pie?
- Do we have the DNA to say "sorry" and mean it?

Does Our Culture Stick When Times Are Tough?

Greg, a worker at Zane's Cycles in Connecticut, volunteered a week of his pay to cover the apology that was extended to a customer from a mistake that he made. His actions proved that Zane's culture was the real thing.

- When things go wrong and a decision needs to be made about how to right a wrong, are these our shining moments?
- Do company values kick in to provide a decision's direction?
- Are people clear on how to do what's right?
- Do they have permission?

Do We Accept Accountability When Things Go Wrong?

Intuit spent $15 million for its TurboTax errors in 2007 when 200,000 customers were unable to get their tax returns in on time because company servers were overloaded. Intuit accepted accountability and fixed the problem swiftly, decisively, and in their customers' best interest.

- When mistakes occur, do we act decisively and in our customers' best interests?
- Do our rescue plans include a commitment to make customers whole, or to just get past the incident?

Can We Suspend the Fear and Say "We're Sorry"?

Dr. Tapas K. Das Gupta, chairman of surgical oncology at the University of Illinois Medical Center, personally met with his patient and her husband to extend his deep apology. He knew the angst they would be feeling upon hearing the news and was prepared to help them through in recovering from his error.

- Are we able to table the "corporate" response and deliver an apology that connects with our customers on a personal level?
- Can we suspend the fear and talk openly and honestly with customers about problems that occur?
- Can we say the words "we're sorry" to our customers?

How Proactive Are We?

Every day, Southwest Airlines convenes a meeting to understand their passengers' experiences from the previous day. They proactively apologize; they don't wait to hear from customers.

- Do we have a proactive recovery plan for knowing what our customers experience?
- When something goes wrong, what actions are set in motion?
- Does our recovery "wow" customers?

Can Our Front Line Rescue Customers?

L.L. Bean's guarantee puts power in the hands of their front line. It gives them freedom to think on their feet and offer options without putting the customer on hold or checking with a manager.

- When a customer calls who is unhappy, does our front line have "permission" to do the right thing?
- Are there options for them to evaluate and exercise using their own good judgment?
- Do we nurture the ability in the front line to think on its feet?

Do We Learn and Change from Our Mistakes?

Remorse is great. But change means you took your customers' experiences to heart. Companies' customers love to make lasting change so no other customers will experience what went wrong. Apologizing well includes a promise to take action to make the problem go away.

- When we say "sorry," how seriously do we take that commitment?
- How strong is our process for ensuring that mistakes do not

It's Now Time for You to Make a Choice.

These brief stories of decisions made by beloved companies have given you a view of the inside of the "clock"—the inner workings that enable a company to become beloved. For these companies, making decisions is how they enable moments of "wow" in a world of customer-experience "vanilla." As you progressed through each chapter, learning about the beloved companies, understanding their decisions, and then contrasting them to your own, you should now know how different or similar your decisions are to theirs.

What draws us to people in our lives are the commonalities that we have with each other. "Golden Rule behaviors," as Colleen Barrett from Southwest Airlines calls them in her Foreword, are our natural tendencies to do the right thing—selfless acts of kindness, in which the reward itself is being able to make decisions that result in treating people the right way. The beloved companies in this book blend commerce with their humanity, they blend their personal lives with their business lives, and they make decisions that are congruent with honoring the person on the other end of the business transaction.

Beloved companies know that in those fleeting moments, they are defined. They know that the actions that come from their decisions indicate what they value. They know that those actions show how much they considered the customer on the other end of the contact, and that those actions reflect back on them—giving customers a glimpse of who they are as people.

Love is irrational. Customer love is a reward for (what some consider) irrational business behavior. Companies who grow because of their bonds with customers do so because they aren't always looking over their shoulders at what each decision will get them. In a world where products and services are available in a hundred variations, these companies get a disproportionate piece of the pie because of how they treat their customers.

Use the decisions in this book to make a choice. Make an active decision about how you will run your business. Decide what story you want told in the marketplace about who you are and what you value. The decisions you make in business measure the depth of your humanity—your ability to apply that simple Golden Rule. How you choose to correct something that goes wrong, how steadfast you are in delivering the goods, ensuring quality, and giving people what they need to do these things all expose what you value. The actions that tumble from these decisions expose the kind of people you are. They tell your story. When you

> **"Use the decisions in this book to make a choice.**
>
> **"Make an active decision about how you will run your business."**

honor your customers and employees, they will tell your story for you. They become an army that markets your products and services every day around the world.

With each shipment you make, with each call, with each support contact, decide what you want your customers to get from you. Decide how you want them to describe you. Choose what story you want them to tell about your products and services. Making it happen begins with how you make decisions. It's about the intent and motivation that guide them. Are you ready?

The Decision Is Yours.

The Final Word
TONY HSIEH, *CEO, Zappos.com*

When I first met Jeanne, I remember thinking that I had come across someone very special. Not only was she clearly passionate about customer service, but she was enthusiastically spreading the word about the power of delivering great service through writing and speaking about it to anyone who would listen. So I invited her to come visit our offices at Zappos, and it was clear from when she first set foot into our building that things just "clicked" for both of us. I'm honored to be asked by her to write a few final closing thoughts.

Decision making, if you don't purposefully guide its direction, can lead your company down a path and to a conclusion you didn't intend. You can unintentionally clip the wings of your people caring for customers. You can take a product, service, or company down the wrong direction. On the other hand, purposeful decisions, informed by how customers live their lives and how your business can improve their lives, can change the course of your business. That's the journey Jeanne has led us through in this book.

By showing us how decisions are made inside loved companies and challenging us with questions to evaluate our own operations, Jeanne gives us a mirror to hold up to ourselves, so we can evaluate our own decision making and the results that come from them.

We are honored to be included in this book. We are continually working on making the Zappos brand be about the very best customer service and the very best customer experience. So, as I read Jeanne's book, I was thinking about her questions and reflecting on what we do here at Zappos.

The key decisions she described in many ways reaffirm our beliefs at Zappos. She recommends that companies make purposeful decisions, believe in their customers, and be real. We made a decision to define, concretely through words, who we are and what we most value. We make our decisions and treat our customers based on our values, and we do so while being as transparent and personal as we can.

One of our core values is to "Build Open and Honest Relationships with Communication." Jeanne talks about "deciding to believe." And we do. We encourage our Customer Loyalty Reps to stay on the phone as long as the customer wants to, as long as we are helping (and WOW-ing) them. A lot of our employees are also now on Twitter, which, like the telephone, is just another means by which we can build more personal relationships with our customers and employees alike. And none of this is done because we're forced to, but because we believe it makes Zappos a better, more positive place for everyone.

The five decisions outlined in this book are reflected in many of our core values and business decisions. From our interview and training process to our employee reviews, they permeate our culture and the way we do business every day. They drive our business decisions at every level. For example, in a world where most companies are looking to cut expenses by reducing the number of customer contacts they have, we decided to take the opposite approach and view each contact as an investment toward building a long-term relationship with the customer, helping us earn loyal customers that grow our business with us. We are excited to have so many customers telling stories about Zappos to their friends and families.

By now, having read this book, you've been through the journey that Jeanne has laid out to evaluate how you make decisions. If you want to be a business that is defined not only by how many new customers you acquire, but also by the number you keep and how passionately they help spread the word about your company, then you're ready for your next decision: What are you going to do now with what you've learned from this book? As Jeanne would say, "The decision is yours."

Acknowledgments

BELIEF is an amazing gift. It made this book a reality. So, here, I want to thank the people who believed. Barbara Cave-Henricks, you were the first. Thank you for reading and being a part of every incarnation of this book. I thank you for being my publicist, but most importantly, for being you. To Bob Levine and Kim Schefler at Levine Plotkin & Menin, you saw this book in its rawest form and believed enough to help me find it a home. Will Weisser, you stretched out your hand from Portfolio and believed that there was a story to tell before you fully knew what it would be. And Adrian Zackheim at Portfolio, the fact that you believed enough to sign on the dotted line humbles me deeply. Jillian Gray, my editor; yours was the strong beating heart at Portfolio that now pounds as rapidly as mine and as passionately for this book. You are far more than an editor; I share what this book has become with you. Allison McLean, thanks so much for your PR passion and the "voice" you are helping to give this book in the marketplace.

Learning at the knee of great leaders is a gift, and while each one helps to mold us into the professional we become, there are very few who also profoundly impact us personally—because they believe. I thank the late Gary Comer, Lands' End founder, for helping me know and feel what it was like to be in a beloved company, so that I could write with knowledge about them.

As we age, what I have found most interesting and rewarding is that the trappings of achievement fall away. What becomes most memorable, and most important, are the paths we took and the people along the way. In writing this book, reaching out and being embraced by Tony Hsieh at Zappos, Colleen Barrett and Fred Taylor at Southwest, Kip Tindell at The Container Store, Chris Zane at Zane's, Sean Murphy and Marc Katz from CustomInk, Brian Scudamore at 1-800-GOT-JUNK, Mike Faith at Headsets.com, and many others confirms and validates what this book is all about. It is the prosperity of the human spirit that fuels the beloved companies. In writing this book, it was my great hope to have found a way to compose a narrative that describes what it feels like to catch lightning in a bottle—because it's a bit like that—being inside of and a part of these great companies. I thank you for your generosity of time and spirit. I hope that I have returned your belief with a description that does you proud.

"When we are young, we learn the golden rule, and then we strap that belief to our back and take it with us into business." I thank my dad and mom for giving me that golden rule foundation and for believing in me my whole life through—no matter what lame-brain thing I conjured up. Linda and Lydia, you are my rocks. And Bill, I am at peace knowing that you always give me the benefit of the doubt, and believe. Finally, women with true friends are the luckiest, only to be superseded by those with friends who read and reread and are read aloud to over and over again. Karyn, Jill, Cyndie, I owe you reading glasses for the rest of your life. Thanks for listening and believing.

Jeanne Bliss

*It is my pleasure to share the contacts, references,
and source notes that made this book a possibility.
Please go to http://www.customerbliss and take a look behind the tab
"Buy the Books." I'll open up my black box behind this book for you
there, as well as provide the sources where the wonderful customer
quotes on the inside cover came from.*

Index

accountability, 14, 31, 50, 59, 142, 144, 145, 189, 191
Acme Humble Pie, 156
ads, pop-up, 57, 58, 80, 181
airlines:
 Southwest Airlines, 20, 53, 62, 88–89, 110, 145, 150, 164, 183, 191, 192
 WestJet, 98, 110, 183
Albrecht, Theo, 110
altruism, 10–11
Amazon.com, 100, 114–15
Amy's Ice Creams, 94, 182
apologizing, 14, 141–72, 189–91
Apple, 136
 iPhone, 143
 Stores, 57–58, 64, 179

Baltimore Business Journal, 20
Bane, Dan, 110
Bangladesh, 30–31
banks:
 Commerce Bank (TD Bank), 128, 187
 Grameen Bank, 30–31
 Umpqua Bank, 70, 122, 177, 180, 186
Baptist Healthcare System, 29
Barrett, Colleen, 88, 145, 164, 192
Baxter International Inc., 168
Bean, Leon Leonwood, 166

being there for customers, 13, 113–39, 145, 185–88
belief, 12, 25–53, 175–78
 apologizing and, 144
Bell, Don, 98
Bennett, Steve, 160
Berra, Yogi, 170
Bible, 10
biorhythmic service, 70
biotechnology, 58
Bleustein, Jeffrey, 50
Body Shop, The, 74
Boone, Garrett, 104
brain, 11, 12
Burke, James, 59–60
BusinessWeek, 132, 166
Byers, Andrew, 148

Carlyle, Thomas, 25
Cathy, Dan, 48
CD Baby, 96, 110, 183
charities, 106, 184
checkout scanners, 57, 102, 184
Chick-fil-A, 48, 178
Churchill, Winston, 141
clarity of purpose, 12–13, 55–83, 178–81
 apologizing and, 145
collaboration and partnership, 36, 50, 132, 178
college students, 136, 188

Collins, Jim, 16–17
Comer, Gary, 3–5, 14–15
Commerce Bank, 128, 187
communication and connection,
    21–22, 96, 100, 102, 104, 106,
    110, 111, 183
Confucius, 10
Conklyn, Elizabeth D., 92
Constantine, Mark, 22, 74, 89, 110
Container Store, The, 36, 104, 110,
    176, 184
Coulombe, Joe, 76, 110
culture, company, 104, 108, 158, 190
customers:
    apologizing to, 14, 141–72,
        189–92
    being there for, 13, 113–39, 145,
        185–88
    belief in, 12, 25–53, 144, 175–78
    communication and connection
        with, 21–22, 96, 100, 102, 104,
        106, 110, 111, 183
    company growth fueled by, 21, 44
    descriptions of, 98, 183
    desires of, 115, 116, 138
    emotions of, 116, 138, 142, 170
    feedback from, 22, 42, 44, 177
    greeting of, 111
    guarantees and, 14–15, 68,
        148–49, 166, 192
    honesty and integrity of, 32
    lives of, 119, 138
    memories of, 62, 136, 181
    at openings, 20–21, 48
    participation in business by,
        19–20, 42, 130, 187
    requests for stores by, 20
    respect for, 108, 185
    trust in, 12, 27, 28, 30, 32, 40, 44,
        52, 175
customer silos, 134, 188
CustomInk, 44, 106, 177, 184

Das Gupta, Tapas K., 162, 191
Davis, Ray, 70
decision-making, 82, 195–96
    democratic, 38, 176
    by employees, 46, 52
decisions, business, 2, 7–23, 173–94
    to believe, 12, 25–53, 144, 175–78
    to be real, 13, 85–112, 145, 182–85
    to be there, 13, 113–39, 145,
        185–88
    clarity of purpose in, 12–13,
        55–83, 145, 178–81
    intent and motivation behind,
        2–3, 5, 8, 14, 15, 22–23, 31–32
    to say sorry, 14, 141–72, 189–92
    story and, 9, 16–17, 22
DeHart, John, 156
desire, 115, 116, 138
dialysis, 168
Disney, Roy, 7
Dreamless, 130
drinking cups, 115–16
Drucker, Peter, 173
DVD rentals, 154, 190

Edward Jones, 132, 188
electronics, 126
emotions, 116, 138, 142, 170
employees, 19
    decision-making by, 46, 52
    flexibility of, 104, 110, 184
    hiring of, 32, 36, 48, 52, 66, 94,
        108, 178, 179, 182
    intelligence of, 32
    leaders and, 91
    product selection by, 42
    purpose and, 82
    sharing information with, 36,
        176
    training of, 46, 66, 104
    trust in, 12, 16, 19, 27, 28, 32, 36,
        46, 52, 175, 177

Faith, Mike, 108, 110, 185
fashion retailers:
    Zappos.com, 21–22, 60–61, 66,
        100, 179, 183, 195–96
    Zara, 21, 120, 186
Fast Company, 38
FedEx, 118
financial services, 30
    Edward Jones, 132, 188
"Fire of Desire, The: A Multisited
    Inquiry in Consumer Passion,"
    115
flexibility, 104, 110, 184
Fortune, 38, 104, 122
Four Seasons, 64, 179
Frost, Robert, 113
Furniture Today, 78

Gap, 21
Genentech, 58–59
Golden Rule, 9–10, 60, 148, 152,
    164, 192, 193
Goodknight, Jim, 132
Good to Great (Collins), 16–17
Gore, Bill, 38
GORE-TEX, 38
Grameen Bank, 30–31
Griffin Hospital, 19, 72
    medical records and, 30, 32, 34,
    175
    parking lot and lobby of, 72,
    180
Griffith, Scott, 136
grocery stores, 32
    Trader Joe's, 20, 21, 42, 57, 58, 76,
        102, 110, 177, 181, 184
    Wegman Food Markets, Inc., 19,
        46, 177
guarantees, 68
    Land's End, 14–15, 148–49
    L.L. Bean, 148–49, 166, 192
Gumby, 104, 110, 184

habit and heart, congruence of, 11
Harley-Davidson, 19, 50, 178
Harley Owners Group, 19
Headsets.com, 108, 110, 182, 185
healthcare, 32
    apologies and, 146–47
    Baptist Healthcare System, 29
    Baxter International Inc., 168
    Griffin Hospital, 19, 30, 34, 72,
        175, 180
    Nurse Next Door, 156, 190
    University of Illinois Medical
        Center, 162, 191
heart and habit, congruence of, 11
Heller, Alan, 168
Henderson, Erlene, 29
hiring, 32, 36, 48, 52, 66, 94, 108,
    178, 179, 182
Homer, 10
Hsieh, Tony, 21, 100, 195–96

IKEA, 20, 78, 181
ikeafans.com, 19–20
innovation, 38, 78
intent, 2–3, 5, 8, 14, 15, 22–23, 31–32
interdependence, 143
International Association of
    Machinists (IAM), 50
Intuit, 160, 191
inventory, 126, 187
iPhone, 143
IRS, 160
Islam, 10

Jobs, Steve, 143
Johnson & Johnson, 59–60, 152, 189
Journal of Consumer Research, 115
junk removal, 118–19

Katz, Marc, 44
Kelleher, Herb, 53, 88
Keller, Helen, 55

Kimberly-Clark, 16–17
Kraemer, Harry, Jr., 168
Kraemer, Henry, 172

labor unions, 50, 178
Land's End, 3–5, 15–16, 27, 89
    guarantee of, 14–15, 148–49
    kids' business of, 89–90
    lattice structure, 38
lawn mowers, 148
lawsuits, 148
    malpractice, 34, 146–47, 162, 175
Lazare, Aaron, 142, 147
leaders, 91, 111
L.L. Bean, 148–49, 166, 192
loans, 30–31
losers, 143
LUSH, 22, 74, 89, 110, 180

McDonald, Timothy B., 162
Macy's, 61
malpractice suits, 34, 146–47, 162,
    175
manufacturing, 32
May, Steve, 122
Mayfield, Lori, 106
Mea Culpa: A Sociology of Apology and
    Reconciliation (Tavuchis), 151
medical records, 30, 32, 34, 175
memory creation, 62, 136, 181
microcredit, 31
military, 92, 182
Miracle on 34th Street, 61
MIT Sloan School of Management, 27
Mohammed, 10
motivation, 2–3, 5, 8, 14, 15, 22–23,
    31–32

Netflix, 154, 190
Neuroscience of Fair Play, The: Why We
    (Usually) Follow the Golden Rule
    (Pfaff), 10–11

Newegg.com, 57, 58, 80, 126, 181, 187
Newman, Simon, 117–18
New York Yankees, 170
Nickell, Jake, 130
Nonzero: The Logic of Human Destiny
    (Wright), 143
Nooyi, Indra, 87–88
Norman, Mark, 136
Nurse Next Door, 156, 190
nurse's aides, 28–29

Odyssey, The (Homer), 10
On Apology (Lazare), 142, 147
1-800-GOT-JUNK?, 118–19
openings, 20–21
    of Chick-fil-A, 48

Paper, Allied-industrial, Chemical,
    and Energy Workers (PACE),
    50
partnership and collaboration, 36,
    50, 132, 178
passion, 36, 50, 91
penny arcades, 128, 187
PepsiCo, 87
Pfaff, Donald, 10–11
pop-up ads, 57, 58, 80, 181
Powanda, Bill, 72
proactive behavior, 145–49, 156,
    164, 190, 191
purpose, 91
    clarity of, 12–13, 55–83, 145,
    178–81

Rackspace, 21, 117–18, 134, 188
real, decision to be, 13, 85–112,
    182–85
    apologizing and, 145
respect, 108, 185
restaurants, 32
    Chick-fil-A, 48, 178
Rettew, Alma, 166

Ritz-Carlton, 64, 179
Roosevelt, Eleanor, 85
Roter, Bruce, 20
rules and regulations, 28, 32, 46, 52, 104, 176, 179

scanners, 57, 102, 184
Scudamore, Brian, 118
self, personal and business, 87
7-Eleven, 76
Shields, John, 76, 110
shipping, 126, 154, 187, 190
Sim, Ken, 156
Smith, Brad, 160
Smith, Darwin, 16–17
Smith, Lois, 17
sorry, saying, 14, 141–72, 189–92
Sorry Works!, 146
Southwest Airlines, 20, 53, 62, 88–89, 110, 150, 183, 191, 192
  apologies from, 145–46, 164
  Morning Overview Meetings at, 145, 164
Starbucks, 136
Steinbrenner, George, 170
story, 9, 16–17, 22, 82, 110, 174–75, 193
students, 136, 188
Study of Spirituality in the Workplace, A, 27
suggestionbox.com, 21–22
supermarkets, 32
  Trader Joe's, 20, 21, 42, 57, 58, 76, 102, 110, 177, 181, 184
  Wegman Food Markets, Inc., 19, 46, 177

Tavuchis, Nicholas, 151
TD Bank, 128, 187
technology, 21, 57, 80, 117, 118, 126
Threadless.com, 19, 130, 187
TIME.com, 164

Tindell, Kip, 36, 104
Torah, 10
Toro Company, 148
Trader Joe's, 20, 21, 42, 58, 76, 102, 110, 177, 181, 184
  scanners and, 57, 102, 184
training, 46, 66, 104
trust:
  belief, 12, 25–53, 144, 175–78
  in customers, 12, 27, 28, 30, 32, 40, 44, 52, 175
  in employees, 12, 16, 19, 27, 28, 32, 36, 46, 52, 175, 177
  reciprocation of, 32, 34, 175
T-shirts:
  CustomInk, 44, 106, 177, 184
  Threadless.com, 19, 130, 187
TurboTax, 160, 191
Twitter, 21, 100, 183, 196
Tylenol, 59, 60, 152, 189

Umpqua Bank, 70, 122, 177, 180, 186
unions, 50, 178
University of Illinois Medical Center, 162, 191
University of Michigan Hospital, 147
University of Zurich, 11
USAA, 92, 182

values, 91
vibe, 76, 181
Vickers, Ken, 102

Walker, Catherine, 156
Wall Street Journal, 164
Waterstone Human Capital, 98
Watson, Gail, 156
Web hosting, 21, 117–18, 134
Wegman, Danny, 46
Wegmans Food Markets, Inc., 19, 46, 177
WestJet, 98, 110, 183

winners, 143, 147
W.L. Gore, 38, 176
Wojcieszak, Doug, 146–47
Women's Wear Daily, 166
Wong, Cynthia, 58–59
Wright, Robert, 143

Yelp.com, 62
Yunus, Muhammad, 30–31

Zane, Chris, 40, 68, 124, 176
Zane's Cycles, 29, 40, 68, 124, 158,
    176, 179, 186, 190
Zappos.com, 21–22, 60–61, 66, 100,
    179, 183, 195–96
Zara, 21, 120, 186
zero-sum games, 143, 147
Zipcar, 19, 136, 188
zipkarma.com, 20

If **CustomInk** were a woman, I would marry her! ▪ I'm in love with **The Container Store**—like I go out of my way to try and find a reason to need to go there. ▪ Oh **IKEA**, how do I love you? . . . let me count the ways. You are my favorite store of all time. ▪ Where else but **Amy's** will employees throw and catch your ice cream before they serve it to you? ▪ **Umpqua Bank**! They even love my dog there. I wouldn't trust my money with anyone else. ▪ In a way, doing business with **CD Baby** feels like hanging out with your best buddy. They just make you feel all warm and fuzzy. ▪ I drive out of my way for **Chick-fil-A**. ▪ Oh, **Apple**, how I love you. You snuck me into your Genius Bar despite being booked 'till the morrow. ▪ When I cut myself shaving, I bleed **Edward Jones Green**, and I wouldn't have it any other way. ▪ The most important phone number in my book is **1-800-GotJunk** ▪ The environment at **Griffin Hospital** is set so that each individual can pull out their inner vitality. ▪ Getting your first **Harley** is like having your first love, sometimes more! ▪ I love dealing with this company, **Headsets.com**. Customer service is top notch. I will keep ordering. ▪ Ok . . . so I LOVE **LUSH**! I have been hooked ever since I first went into a store in London. . . . The staff here is supercool and camp! ▪ I'm in love. The kind of love that makes you weak in the knees and excited to be alive. . . . The Web site is phenomenal and very user-friendly. I LOVE **Newegg.com**!! ▪ It's not the **Netflix** refund I'm happy about, it's the principle of the matter. They had issues and acknowledged them. More than you can say for most companies. ▪ **Nurse Next Door** really cares about their clients and is always willing to go the extra mile! ▪ I've been a **Rackspace** customer for about a year and a half, and I've been absolutely NUTS about them the entire time! ▪ Reason Number One I love **Southwest Airlines**—